But How'd I Get in There in the First Place?

Talking to Your Young Child About Sex

DEBORAH M. ROFFMAN

PERSEUS
PUBLISHING

Cataloging-in-Publication Data is available from the Library of Congress
ISBN 0-7382-0572-9

Perseus Publishing is a member of the Perseus Books Group.
Find us on the World Wide Web at http://www.perseuspublishing.com
Perseus Publishing books are available at special discounts for bulk purchases in the U.S. by corporations, institutions, and other organizations. For more information, please contact the Special Markets Department at the Perseus Books Group, 11 Cambridge Center, Cambridge, MA 02142, or call (800) 255-1514 or (617) 252-5298, or e-mail j.mccrary@perseusbooks.com.

Text design by Jeff Williams
Set in 11-point ACaslon Regular

First printing, March 2002

1 2 3 4 5 6 7 8 9 10—05 04 03 02

To Goldie and Mike

Who taught me about sex?
Not my father or my mother.
So how did I learn?
They loved one another.

—ANONYMOUS

Contents

Why a Book About Sexuality for Parents of Young Children?

In Baltimore, Maryland, where I live and work, I have a very unique nickname: The Sex Lady.

Don't misunderstand. It's not as if you'd pass me on the street, take a quick glance, and instantly say to yourself—"Oh, I'll bet that's The Sex Lady." It's not *that* kind of nickname.

Sex Lady is actually a handle many of my students call me by. (I hope I'm not getting myself in deeper here.) As the person who comes to their school off and on throughout the school year to teach sexuality education, I'm not always recognized at first, because it may have been quite a while since students last saw me in the building. "Hey, I remember her," I'll hear them say to someone a few paces behind me down the hallway. "Wasn't that the sex lady?"

Well, eventually it's caught on and become somewhat official. I can't really say that I mind it (my own children, not to mention my husband, on the other hand, are another story). In fact, it always makes me feel good to know that my students remember me, and that maybe it means they also remember some of the things we talked about in our classes.

As I've been writing this new book during the past year, friends and colleagues have asked what this one is about. "It's a book for

1

parents of young children," I report. Many have looked momentarily perplexed. "Oh," they finally say, "I guess this one's not about sex."

Each time this has happened, I've become more convinced than ever about how much a book on this topic is needed. Even though sexuality educators like myself have been trying for decades to help everyone understand that people are sexual beings from birth on—and that sexuality education, therefore, begins at the very moment we are born—it seems we have a long way yet to go.

Though there are many facets of my job, one of my favorites is working with parents of very young children. What an opportunity—to help young parents be able to "see" and understand how to actively nurture their children's healthy sexual and gender development from the very beginning! That's my first hope in writing this book.

My second is to help everyone—parents, caretakers, grandparents, teachers, and anyone else who interacts in an ongoing way with children—learn to relax about the process of sexual learning. So many of us anticipate this process with anxiety, yet truthfully, educating children and adolescents about sexuality can be downright fascinating—and even great fun!

It's also a process that's much more manageable and predictable than you might think. Years ago, after listening to hundreds of parents talk about their experiences, I concluded that children themselves, even the youngest of them, are our best teachers. Typically, and spontaneously, they will begin at about age four to ask a predictable sequence of questions about their origins that can lead us gradually and comfortably to thoroughly age-appropriate conversations about sex and reproduction: *Where did I come from? How did I get out of there?* And, finally, if you're like most parents, the big one: *How did I get in there in the first place?* If you're aware that these questions are coming and understand *why* they're so predictable and developmentally on target, I know you'll feel much more prepared and relaxed. And, that, I hope, will set the stage for many, many more important—and enjoyable!—conversations to come.

1

From Daunting to Doable

Eight young women sit around a coffee table in Rebecca's newly decorated family room, admiring the changes. They chat about children, work, and extended families. Rebecca interrupts to say it's time to get started and introduces me as the speaker for this evening's mothers' group program.

The conversation stops and the women are immediately focused. Tonight's topic is one they've really been anticipating. I hardly begin my introduction before the avalanche of questions begins:

"My little boy touches himself *all the time!* What do I do?"

"What about playing 'doctor' with other children. Is that okay or what?"

"I want to tell my daughter the proper words for her body parts, but what if she goes around telling other children?"

"How about nudity? My husband and I are really uninhibited. Is that good—or is that bad?"

"I have an eight-year-old, too, very curious. What if he asks me questions in front of my four-year-old?"

"Billy wants to know what's in my tampon box. What do I say?"

It has become clear that these women have much more in common than being parents of rambunctious four-year-olds. They are well educated, competent, and extremely self-aware. All of them take their children's health and well-being seriously, and they are compulsively proactive when it comes to their care. They share a fierce determination to become the very best parents they can possibly be.

But when it comes to the topic of sexuality, they feel as if they are flying totally by the seat of their pants.

I take a moment to share these reflections with the group. Each of the women nods, suddenly aware of their collective but uncharacteristic confusion. It seems obvious, I say, that the issue they most need to deal with is not so much sexuality as why the *subject* of sexuality is so darned hard to get their usually sensible heads around in the first place. Why is this topic so different? Once they get to the bottom of that question, I promise, the daunting will become much more doable.

How Did This Topic Get to Be *So* Tough?

Many years ago, when I first began to travel around the country to train educators, counselors, and other professionals to teach sexuality education, I was intrigued by the very same contradiction that struck me about the young women in Rebecca's family room. Despite long years of training and experience, these professionals had one thing in common: They hadn't a clue about how even to think about the process of sexuality education, not even a shred of an idea about where to start. Without a lot of help, they simply were unable to apply to this issue what they already knew unfailingly about many other subjects. In short, what they shared in common is that somehow they had lost their good common sense.

Many parents, even those who are extremely capable and proactive, act and feel the same way. When faced with a sexual question or situation, we often come up with the same great big "Duh!"—a previously facile mind suddenly empty of understanding, explanation, or creative ideas—particularly, it seems, when it comes to the youngest of our children. And, of course, that blank reaction in itself can make us feel all the more uncertain and out of control, and even less able to cope.

If these reactions sound all too familiar, take heart: It means there are common causes, and therefore common solutions, for our bewilderment. Here are some of the more common ones:

Missing Role Models

Whenever I speak with a new group of adults, I always ask how many of them grew up with parents or, for that matter, any adults in their lives—teachers, aunts, uncles, grandparents, friends of the family—who were able to talk with them comfortably and honestly about sexuality. Typically the number of hands that go up is pathetically small, usually no more than 10 to 20 percent. In a large group of a hundred or more adults, it is stunning to see how many grew up with virtually no role models to demonstrate what a grownup looks and sounds like when he or she is communicating capably and responsibly with a young person about sexuality. Even more telling—especially for parents struggling with their toddlers and preschool children over these issues—is how few of us, if any, received any kind of early instruction about this topic in school. Most of us can remember nothing whatsoever taught about sex or reproduction prior to the fourth or fifth grade. No wonder we are at such a loss! How can we reasonably expect ourselves automatically to know what to do or how to talk with our young children on these matters when we cannot see or hear ourselves, either as the teacher or the student, reflected in our relationships with them?

Baseline Anxiety

I do not mean to suggest that we learned nothing about sexuality as young children: It is wrong to assume that children are learning only when others are talking directly to them or consciously bringing a particular topic to their attention. Children—especially young children—learn most of what they come to know through a much more indirect and moment-by-moment process of observation and assimilation. As they go about their daily business, all of the time and through all of their senses, they continuously draw in physical, social, emotional, and factual data from their surroundings that little by little help shape how they come to see and understand their world.

An example: When I was a child, any discussion of sexuality was taboo in my family. I certainly wasn't told this rule outright, since that would have required someone actually to speak about it! So I must have learned it, or rather *intuited* it, gradually over a long period of time. Whenever the topic of sexuality happened to come up, incidentally or accidentally, I must have sensed the abrupt shift in the ambience of my family life. Suddenly someone would blush, crack a joke, give a look, lower his eyes, clear his throat, or try to change the subject. While moments before we all might have been conversing naturally and comfortably, there would be a sudden feeling of tension and threat in the air. I'm certain that I did not like the way that felt at all, especially since I also knew I wasn't to ask what everyone was so tense and threatened about. I knew I had no way to make it go away. So, to keep the threat as small as possible, I learned to enter into an unspoken pact with my parents in a generations-old conspiracy of silence and denial, to keep my family and myself emotionally "safe" from this "dangerous" topic.

Without knowing it, I think many of us carry this baseline feeling of anxiety with us into adulthood as a learned association to the subject of sex and sexual learning. Then, as young parents, we may make unconscious or subconscious connections to these earlier experiences and cause ourselves to feel inappropriately anxious or nervous when—inevitably—the subject happens to come up around our own children. Unless we can identify and reexamine these reactions, we may continue to experience the topic as threatening in irrational ways. We may even find that these unresolved feelings trigger the signs of a classic biological stress response: We may feel suddenly compelled to *flee* (change the subject at all costs), *fight* (get angry at whoever brought it up), or totally *freeze* (our mind goes blank and we can't think of a thing to say). Hence, the big "Duh!"

Cultural Attitudes

But from where, exactly, do these irrational associations and anxieties originate? Even in the twenty-first century—even in our increasingly sex-saturated society—Americans are very much a product of an earlier and more puritanical past. In our parents' generations and certainly in their parents' and grandparents' before them, ad infinitum, talking about sex in public and even in private was not only considered inappropriate; in the presence of children it was considered potentially *dangerous*. The old adage "if you tell them about it, they'll do it" was the prevailing folk wisdom. Conversely, the way to keep children safe—and chaste—was to make sure the information didn't surface "too early." Children were to be kept ignorant and "innocent" as long as possible, lest "knowing" would lead to "doing." Although these attitudes are centuries old, and modern life and the social, cultural, and media pressures brought to bear on young people are vastly different today, in most schools and in many families silence and evasion are still all too common.

Post-Sixties Sensibilities

But wait a minute, what about the sixties? What about the Sexual Revolution? Why are we *still* so tongue-tied?

In many ways, I'm convinced the "Sexual Revolution" actually has worked *against* parents. (Truthfully, I believe what transpired in the 1960s was more of a revolt than a revolution, since so many unhealthy attitudes remain with us.) First of all, while people may have been "liberated" from previous restrictive rules about sexual behavior, *changes in behavior do not necessarily signal changes in fundamental attitudes, feelings, and beliefs.* As a culture and as individuals we've not yet worked through our centuries-old baseline discomfort and anxiety associated with the topic of sexuality, and with talking about it.

Among the most obvious signs of this today are the many adults who come to parenthood assuming they are very modern in their attitudes, only to be surprised and chagrined by the embarrassment or discomfort they experience as they confront issues of sexuality in the family. Even more determined by this unexpected response to be "sex-positive" in raising their children—unlike the way they perceive they were raised—many tend to overreact in the opposite direction. On the one hand, they become so fearful of projecting any kind of negativity, they're unable to set appropriate limits around their children's sexual curiosity or behavior. On the other, never having worked through the "knowing leads to doing" anxiety they may have absorbed as young children from their own parents, they may find they are also afraid to come across as *too* sex-positive. Ironically, this confusion, anxiety, and discomfort may cause parents to end up sending their children the very same negative and/or mixed messages they were so determined to avoid in the first place. It's not surprising at all that every one of the scenarios painted by the moms in the beginning of this chapter reveals this pervasive tension and worry over saying *too much and too little*, being *too open or too closed*, reacting *too early or too late*.

Five Principles to Parent By

Parents are certainly right to want to get it right and to believe that the early years are crucial to the formation of healthy sexual attitudes. Contrary to what our intuition may tell us, however, concerns about *quantity of knowledge*—questions about when, how much, how little to tell—are not the correct ones to place at the heart of the process: It's the *quality of the communication* we share with our their children, not the quantity of information we give or hold back, that matters. Even more confusing, inviting quality communication with a child in our care may require accepting a set of approaches that may in fact seem *counterintuitive* to some of our most basic parenting hunches and instincts.

What parents need today is a new kind of blueprint to guide them in the process of figuring out and meeting their children's learning needs, one that makes sense in terms of both normal, healthy sexual development and the realities of today's world. Here are what I consider to be *five essential sexual learning principles*, located at the base of that new foundation, that we will revisit in many forms throughout this book.

1. Sexual knowledge is good. Talking about sexuality is good, and good for children. Acquiring sexual literacy is an essential goal for children and adolescents in today's world.

2. Children are born ignorant of sexual knowledge, but they are active learners from birth on. In the process of their normal intellectual, social, and emotional development, and as they continuously absorb information from the world around them, they will begin to form and pose questions spontaneously that can easily lead adults to provide age-appropriate information about sexuality. If an adult responds in a welcoming fashion, those questions will continue, in a predictable manner and sequence, through childhood and even well into adolescence.

3. Factual knowledge about the topic of sexuality is vast and growing constantly, and it is easily accessed in multiple ways in our society. Children are capable of learning sexual information in a gradual and ongoing fashion, beginning at about

the age of one year, when they acquire language and begin to learn the names for their sexual body parts. Especially when children are young, it is best that they learn this information from the immediate adults in their lives, particularly parents and teachers; absent their involvement, children will learn from others.

4. Sexual knowledge, like all knowledge, is powerful. Used carefully and deliberately, it is the cornerstone of safe, healthy, moral conduct. Research consistently demonstrates that children who grow up in families where sexuality is openly discussed grow up *healthier* (e.g., they make healthier decisions) and *slower* (e.g., they are more likely to delay sexual activity).

5. Sexuality is an essential part of life, and sexual knowledge is essential to a responsible life. The immediate adults in a child's life are morally responsible for passing on sexual knowledge to children and adolescents in an informed, deliberate, and timely fashion.

These principles are meant to accomplish three things at once: to allay misplaced anxieties that cause us to lose our common sense about the processes of healthy sexual development; to reinforce the crucial role of parents as the primary sexuality educators of their children; and to communicate unequivocally that children are not the *objects* of our educational efforts but rather *our partners* in a joint educational adventure. As we will see time and again throughout this book, children are not empty vessels that adults control by choosing to leave empty or make full; they are whole and active partners in the teaching/learning process.

Five Universal Needs

After many years of experience—as a teacher, parent, and parent educator—I noticed something significant and reassuring: *Whenever children present us with sexual issues or situations—regard-*

*less of their age—they express one or more of just five easily identifiable,
developmentally based needs.* Ever since, I've been encouraging parents to acquire a new and helpful kind of developmental "lens" in
analyzing and responding to sexuality-related situations as they
present themselves in family life. Particularly when it comes to
topics as potentially anxiety-provoking as sexuality, this "five-needs
paradigm" helps parents stay in touch with their common sense
and good judgment. Instead of automatically saying to themselves,
"Oh, no! Not SEX!" they learn to think instead: "Now, even
though it looks and feels like it, this question (or situation) isn't
fundamentally about sex. It's really about one or more of the five
core developmental needs that are common to all questions and
situations. All I need to do is think in terms of those needs, and
I'll know how to respond, or at least how to think about what I
should do."

The first step in using the "five needs paradigm" is to acquire a
thorough understanding of the needs (their presentation follows).
The second is to become skilled in recognizing each of the needs
as they arise in different children and at different ages and stages
of development. Finally, the third is to learn to draw confidently on
a cadre of specific parenting skills that are matched to each of the
developmental needs. After we've identified the five core needs
below, we'll return to the parenting scenarios presented at the
beginning of the chapter to practice the steps of correctly identifying the child's need or needs and then matching them with the
most helpful and developmentally supportive responses.

Affirmation: Children and adolescents need adults to recognize
the ongoing nature of sexual development and to positively affirm
each particular stage of normal sexual development.

Information giving: Children and adolescents need ready sources
of factual knowledge and concepts about sexuality and to have
information presented in ongoing and age-appropriate ways.

Values clarification: Children and adolescents need adults to clearly share their personal values, and as children become more socially aware, they need adults to clarify and interpret competing values and values systems in the surrounding culture.

Limit setting: Children and adolescents need adults to create a healthy and safe environment by clearly stating and consistently reinforcing age-appropriate rules and limits.

Anticipatory guidance: Children and adolescents need adults to help them learn how to avoid or handle potentially harmful situations and to rely, when necessary, on themselves to make responsible and healthy choices.

Now we're ready to match children's *needs* to some possible appropriate adult *responses*. We'll do a somewhat cursory job here, then provide much more information and guidance in later chapters.

My little boy touches himself all the time! What do I do? The mom in this situation learned to see her son's explorations as a normal expression of curiosity that is very common among four-year-olds and about which she need not be alarmed. *(Affirmation)* She also learned that part of her confusion arose because there was a second need in operation in this situation, the need for *limit setting*. The two needs required two different kinds of responses. She needed both to *affirm* her child's feelings (by saying something like, "I can see that you really like touching your penis because it feels good when you do that") and also to *set a limit* around his behavior ("but touching your genitals is private behavior"). If the child isn't ready yet intellectually to comprehend the concept of privacy, she'll want to try another approach, perhaps choosing to ignore the behavior until he or she is older and capable of understanding.

What about playing "doctor" with other children. Is that okay or what? As we'll discuss further in Chapter 5, young children very commonly engage in a variety of activities that involve looking at and touching other children's genitals. Often, adults misinterpret this kind of situation, inappropriately projecting adult motivations or behaviors onto the situation ("They are trying to have sex!"). Once again, the parent needs to understand and *affirm* the children's motivation (curiosity, pleasurable physical sensations) and experience (enjoying a fun game). Then he or she can proceed to sort out the *limit setting* implications that the situation might call for. Since in this kind of situation, obviously, another child or other children are involved, the issue of *values clarification* may also come into play (How will the parents of the other children involved possibly feel about this kind of activity?) and help shape the parent's response. *Anticipatory guidance* may also eventually become an important need, as the parent finds it necessary to discuss with the child the behavior that's expected when she or he is playing at other children's homes.

I want to tell my daughter the proper words for her body parts, but what if she goes around telling other children? In this kind of situation, it's the parents who need to do some hard thinking about values in order to discover what is most important to them. Do they wish to *affirm* their child's needs for correct and complete information, or do they want to *set limits* around the information they are willing to provide because of larger social issues and concerns? It's perhaps the first of many times when parents will need to learn how to balance their own family's standards against the realities of a society that encompasses a very broad spectrum of values and attitudes about sexuality.

How about nudity? My husband and I are really uninhibited. Is that good—or is that bad? Nudity in the family is another topic around which there exists a broad range of opinions and attitudes in society, and one that, for most families, provokes confusion and uncertainty at some point or another. Whenever a question or concern about nudity arises, it's almost always an opportunity for personal *values clarification* and for knowing when and how to *set comfortable limits* that make sense for both children and parents. If your family's attitudes are pretty open, be aware that sooner or later either you or your child will probably reach a point where a desire for greater modesty or privacy will naturally emerge. You'll probably just sense this because of a new kind of look or glance, or a sudden need for distance or space, or perhaps the hint of physical or emotional tension in the air. Sometimes children will let you know outright by telling you directly that they want more privacy or by making an abrupt change in their customary behavior (like suddenly closing the bathroom door or wearing a bathrobe). It will be important to respect these signals—or your own sudden or growing discomfort—by matter-of-factly shifting the family's rules or *limits* to provide for greater privacy. Many parents will want a larger zone of privacy from the very beginning, and that's fine too.

I have an eight-year-old, too, very curious. What if he asks me questions in front of my four-year-old? The parent's concern in this situation revolves around the huge issue of "age appropriateness," a source of much confusion and consternation for American adults, whose own sexual learning typically was replete with huge gaps and holes as they were growing up. Lurking also is what I like to call the "age-appropriate demons"—those scary "old tapes" in the back of our minds admonishing us relentlessly that "too much information too soon" could be problematic if not downright dangerous. Truthfully, most of the time, these kinds of conversations can proceed normally and quite casually; whatever the younger child isn't interested in or can't comprehend just yet will whiz right by as he or she finds something much more interesting to pay attention to.

Billy wants to know what's in my tampon box. What do I say? This is a great example of the kinds of situations that can make the normally facile mind of a perfectly competent adult go "Duh!" To us this question is about a box containing an object that is placed inside a sexual organ, and therefore, at least indirectly, the question has something to do with sex. To the child, this question is about a box, period (pardon the pun). Once we've figured that out the rest is easy. How would we answer any other question about what might be inside an interesting looking box that caught our child's attention—let's say, a box of tissue? Instead of blank nothingness, we'd for sure be able to come up with a huge and creative array of possible responses, from the very specific ("It contains soft pieces of paper that you wipe your nose with when you have a cold") to the very general ("It's stuff from the drug store"). We'd pick the answer that seemed best to fit the situation, and that would be that.

Chapters to Come

In Chapter 2, we'll define the topic of "human sexuality" in its broadest sense as a way of understanding the concept of lifelong sexual development. We'll come to appreciate the differences between the issues of "sex education" (didactic education about sexual behavior per se and the relevant "facts of life") and "sexuality education" (the sum total of formal and informal learning about who we are as sexual people).

Chapters 3, 4, and 5 will provide a multitude of very practical strategies for responding to the myriad tough questions and perplexing situations around issues of sexuality that toddlers and young children often present.

In Chapters 6 and 7, we'll move our focus outside of the home and enter the worlds of early childhood and early elementary education. We'll explore the many ways in which schools and families can work *together* to support our children's healthy sexual growth and development. Finally, Chapter 8 will offer a host of other resources for families and schools.

2

How Children Learn About Sexuality

Ask any seasoned sexuality educator to identify the one question that parents ask most often, and you'll be told without hesitation: "When do I bring it up, how do I explain it, and how much do I say?" (often with the subtext "And how long can I put it off altogether!").

The "it," of course, is sex and its role in reproduction. For most parents, this particular focus as the starting place in their thinking about sexuality education makes perfect sense: It's a direct corollary of how we in American culture tend to define the concept of sexuality and how we tend to think about the way children learn.

In most people's minds, the word *sexuality* is basically a longer version of the word *sex*. The average person thinks of sexuality as encompassing the totality of topics and experiences that have to do with the act of sex or, more specifically, the act of sexual intercourse: male and female anatomy and physiology, erections, ejaculation, sperm, eggs, conception, sexual response, pleasure, orgasms, birth control, sexually transmitted infections, and the like. When it comes to topics that might be included in sexuality education in middle or high schools, the list probably would be very similar and might also include subjects like abstinence, rape, sexual assault, sexual decision-making and values, relationships, love, marriage, and family life.

In truth, this kind of thinking is exceptionally narrow. Defining the topic of sexuality as being simply about sex is like defining American history as being about, let's say, World War II, the invention of the automobile, or the signing of the Declaration of Independence. Each is an essential piece of the big picture but only a relatively small part of the whole. Even our linguistic habit of using the word *sex* as shorthand for sexual intercourse is very narrow and misleading, since there are a great variety of ways that people can "have sex" or engage in sexual activity. When we speak this way we confuse ourselves—and children who may be listening—into thinking that genital intercourse is the only *real* or *important* kind of sex. (You may recall a recent presidential scandal that elucidated many of the problems associated with this kind of thinking and speaking!)

If we take another look at the questions posed at the beginning of the chapter, we'll find another assumption common to the way adults think about sexuality education. Even in today's sex- and media-saturated society, where sexual content, imagery, and references can be seen and heard virtually everywhere, many parents continue to assume nonetheless that they are in total control of their children's sexual upbringing: Unless they've initiated a direct conversation or responded to a direct question, their reasoning goes, their children have learned nothing. As explained in Chapter 1, children learn most of what they come to know by observation and assimilation, not didactic conversation, and sexuality—defined broadly—is no exception.

What Is Sexuality?

A narrow view of sexuality and sexual learning—as something isolated and separate from the rest of life—diminishes our understanding of how central these issues are to our children's overall growth and development. Conversely, broadening our notion of the multiple dimensions of sexuality helps us to understand our multiple roles in raising sexually healthy children.

Just what are these "dimensions" of sexuality?

Who We Are: Identity

It was Mary Calderone, founder of the Sexuality Information and Education Council of the United States (SIECUS), who first pointed out that sexuality has much more to do with *who we are* than *what we do*. One way of understanding this concept is to realize that human sexuality—and therefore sexuality education—is essentially not about *body parts* and what they can do; it is about the thinking, feeling, valuing, experiencing, growing, changing, decision-making, relationship-building *person* who is attached to them. Envisioned so broadly, sexuality encompasses utterly every facet of human experience connected to who we are as male or female people.

Who We Are Becoming: Development

All human beings are the product of continuous growth and development. Since sexuality is an aspect of our total selves, it too grows and changes as we do. Throughout our lives, we continually experience new sexual and reproductive challenges and stages. Although the dramatic changes that occur during puberty are among the most concrete and dramatic examples of early sexual development, as we'll come to understand, there are many important benchmarks in infancy and childhood as well.

How We Experience Our Bodies: Sensuality

Our sensuality has to do with how we experience and regard our bodies; quite obviously, then, it is a natural and integral component of being a sexual person. How freely we allow ourselves to give, receive, and enjoy sexual arousal and pleasure; our body image and level of comfort (or discomfort) with our body's appearance, sensations, and functions; our assessment of our sexual desirability and our physical attractiveness are all part of our sexual self-concept. And, perhaps the most basic of all aspects of sensuality and sexuality is our primal need to be touched, caressed, and held.

How We Experience Closeness: Intimacy

Physical intimacy is of course central to sexual fulfillment and satisfaction. It is also the flip side of emotional intimacy. Learning to integrate the physical and emotional aspects of intimacy, closeness, and sexual desire is one of the most complex and enduring challenges of adolescence and adulthood. Although we may not realize it—because of our reluctance to understand and accept infants and children as sexual beings—healthy adult intimacy is rooted in the close relationships and loving experiences between infants and caretakers.

What We Stand For: Values

Sexual behavior is a powerful force in people's lives. Ethical sexual conduct requires careful thought about one's moral values and choices—especially in a society that continually sends sensationalized and confusing messages about the nature and meaning of sexual behavior. For adolescents and young adults, "right" decision making requires strong relationship skills, a healthy respect for self and others, and a consistent inner core of attitudes, feelings, beliefs, and values.

How We Care for Ourselves and Others: Health

Health is far more than the absence of disease or dysfunction. As the World Health Organization asserts, it encompasses optimal health and well-being along all of life's dimensions—physical, social, emotional, intellectual, and spiritual. And yet, in thinking about raising sexually healthy children in a society whose attention is focused almost exclusively on the genital aspects of sexuality, it becomes difficult to see beyond the specter of HIV and other sexually transmitted infections, teenage pregnancy, and premature sexual involvement. Just as health involves far more than disease prevention, sexuality education entails much more than sexual "damage control." It truly is education for lifelong fulfillment and satisfaction.

How Young Children Learn

An anecdote I was told a couple of years ago provides a marvelous—yet frightening—window into the minds of young children and how they learn.

The story was told by Renee Soulis, a gifted educator who delivers wonderful presentations and workshops about alcohol and other drugs all across the country in her work for Freedom from Chemical Dependency (FCD) Educational Services. One year, Renee was invited to pilot a program at the early elementary school level, an age group with which FCD had not previously worked. As she prepared for her first sessions, she decided to proceed very gradually in order to acquire a firsthand sense of the children's knowledge and interest level. She began by asking two simple questions.

The first question was, "Tell me, please, in your experience, what do children drink for lunch?"

"Milk!" "Juice!" "Soda!" "Water!" "Punch!" the children were only too happy to share.

"Okay, great," she said. "Now, tell me what you've noticed that adults drink."

Well, even Renee, a well-seasoned and shock-proof educator who's worked with tens of thousands of kids and adults, was not at all prepared for what she heard next.

"Piña colada," "Bloody Marys," "chardonnay," "black Russians," "Coors Light," the children called out confidently and matter-of-factly (as if to say, when are you going to get to the hard questions?).

As the conversation continued, Renee was increasingly stunned. Not only did these children know the names for all kinds of alcoholic beverages, they could even match up what kind of drinks were most appropriately consumed in conjunction with what particular kinds of activities. Moms sip rum and coke when they play bridge and margaritas when they go out to lunch, while dads order martinis. Men drink huge cups of beer at the ballpark and out of flasks at a football game. Gin and tonics go with the beach, wine with meals, and hot toddies are essential after skiing. Said one little girl, "and adults drink when they take off their coat, too."

"What do you mean by that?," inquired Renee, very puzzled.

"Well," she explained, "when friends of my parents come over for dinner or a party, my mom or my dad always says, 'Hi! We're so glad you could come. Can I take your coat for you, and what would you like to drink?'"

As the saying goes, "children learn what they live," even about subjects that we might consider to be for and about "adults only." Whatever is in our world is in their world, unless we take very conscious and deliberate steps to keep them separate. In the twenty-first century, particularly in media-driven cultures like the United States', when it comes to so-called adult behaviors like drinking—and like sex—the line between the adult and nonadult world is becoming barely visible.

There are plenty of external stimuli that project issues of sexuality prematurely into our children's lives, in ways that require our attention and even our vigilance. That topic will be addressed thoroughly in later chapters. But let's be clear that the point is not to keep sex or sexuality out of sight and mind because children are "too young." The point is to recognize—and nurture—the healthy and developmentally appropriate ways in which *it already is and should be in their lives.* To understand how, we'll need to revisit the six dimensions of sexuality and sexual learning.

Identity

The biggest component of our sexuality—our "genderality," as I like to call it—refers to all the ways that each of us thinks, feels, and acts because of our gender. Who we are as males or females is a fundamental part of our total personality and deep-rooted sense of identity. In fact, it is arguably the most fundamental.

As everyone knows, the piece of news anticipated most eagerly at the time of a baby's birth (if not before) is the pronouncement of her or his biological gender. In truth, the perception of a baby's gender remains a purely biological issue for only a split second in time. Instantaneously, thousands upon thousands of personal, interpersonal, and cultural associations connected to the concepts of "boyness" and "girlness" will coalesce and inform the ways in which she or he will be perceived and treated by others. Projected onto the blank screen of an infant's psyche and reinforced by every single interaction every single day thereafter, these perceptions and expectations will shape profoundly how the child will come to see her- or himself. Therefore, what began as a simple, direct statement of *biology* eventually becomes an indirect and powerful determiner of *identity.*

Some researchers and psychologists argue that there are significant brain variations present at birth that may account for later male and female differences. They believe that these inborn traits themselves condition parents to respond to infants in particular ways, which they then improperly interpret as culturally stereotypical. (Other scientists maintain that the infant brain is still immature and quite "plastic" and that any small inborn differences are easily overridden by early environmental conditioning.) And everyone knows a child or children whose behavior from birth—sometimes despite deliberate parental efforts to the contrary—is "all boy" or "all girl," that is, their behavior and personality just seem naturally and effortlessly to exhibit and perfectly fit traditional male or female roles.

Scientists no doubt will continue to unravel more fully these point-counterpoint relationships between nature and nurture. There is no question, however, that there are a multitude of subtle yet potent differences (as well as many more obvious and stereotypical ones) in how we relate and thereby shape the lives of male versus female infants and toddlers according to our learned perceptions and expectations regarding gender. It is difficult to believe that these rudimentary experiences won't in themselves become powerful precursors of later gender differences—in interests, hobbies, abilities, styles, roles, traits, personality, and so forth—of the kinds often explained away as self-evident, folk-wisdom proof that "boys will be boys" and "girls will be girls." There'll be more about this in Chapter 5, but right now, just to prove the power of gender role messages for yourself, walk into your child's room, look around, and do a quick mental calculation of the number of objects that would *not* be there if he or she had been born of the other gender. Better yet, just count the number of things that would remain. You'll then have a good measure of what your child has been learning day by day, month by month, for years in "gender school" and a better understanding of how fundamental gender is to basic identity.

Development

In Chapter 1, we identified the five universal needs of children and adolescents as they grow toward sexual maturity. The first and most important of these needs is for *affirmation,* the ability of the immediate adults in their lives to recognize the ongoing nature of sexual development and to positively affirm each particular stage of normal growth.

For parents whose picture of sexuality education is braving the "big talk" at age six or seven, learning about periods and wet dreams when you're eleven, or enduring a birth control or AIDS lecture in high school, it will be next to impossible to imagine what a sexuality "course" might look like for a newborn. But, if we accept that sexuality is part of life and come to understand how babies begin to learn about life from the very moment it begins, the "curriculum" begins to take shape.

The lessons children learn during the first years of life lay the foundation for all of the monumental physical, social, emotional, and intellectual changes ahead. In the earliest months, most of the learning that occurs will transpire out of the infant's daily interactions with immediate caretakers. The first of these life lessons will be about the issue of trust. As parents and others provide sustenance, warmth, touch, rest, and physical comfort in ongoing, predictable ways, we "teach" that the world is fundamentally a loving, safe, and responsive place. Precisely because of this secure base—and in concert with the steady acquisition of language and mobility—the protective cocoon of infancy will eventually render itself obsolete. Our helpless infant will become the confident explorer, ready to take on a vastly enlarged physical and intellectual world.

Whether we realize it or not, we are also providing a foundation for the child's later sexual life. The pleasure and relaxation that infants come to associate with our loving touch and our warm and comforting presence will become their first and most important lessons in physical intimacy. We can also enhance these good feelings and this positive foundation by consciously showing acceptance and approval of children's body parts and functions, including the sexual parts and their nearby neighbors, the urinary and digestive parts. If we can maintain the same affirming yet matter-of-fact attitude toward these parts and functions as we do all others—at bath time, while changing diapers or applying medicine or lotions, or when baby happens to touch or rub on her or his genitals—we help them to understand and accept their bodies as a positive and integrated whole.

While infants and toddlers are exquisitely attuned to human contact and other sources of stimulation in their external environment, they are also shaped by an internal timetable of development that provokes learning from the inside out. Their bodies—always accessible, always changing—provide a living, breathing classroom and a constant source of self-knowledge. At birth, bodies are an immediate and constant source of multiple sensations—pleasurable and not—particularly in and around each of the various orifices. Later, the sounds that bodies can make (gurgles, burps, coos, flatulence) and the products they create (tears, urine, feces, saliva, mucus) will also attract great interest and attention. Just as the primary caretaker's world revolves around the infant's bodily needs, so does the infant's, only more so. Their body is them.

As babies' thought processes advance, they gradually develop an intellectual awareness of their body as a concrete whole that is separate from other people's bodies. They also come to understand that their body is *a part of* who they are, not equal to who they are, and they become capable of observing it and thinking about it, not just experiencing it. Eventually they are able to step back far enough mentally from the experience of their body to appreciate and conceptualize it in terms of its physical attributes—particularly its size, shape, parts, and functions. This awareness invites inevitable questions about what things are called, what they do, and how they work and inevitable comparisons with the size, shape, parts, and functions of other people's bodies. And, of course, their sexual parts will be no exception.

How we respond to our children's natural curiosity about sexual parts and functioning, and about gender differences, will teach at least as much as any particular factual information we may impart.

A shocked look or suddenly embarrassed tone of voice, for example, teaches a very different lesson than a business-as-usual, matter-of-fact reply. If these kinds of out-of-the-ordinary reactions recur over time, the child will learn, or at least sense, that there is something different and maybe even suspect about this particular region of his or her living classroom. It is to be treated differently and thought about differently than all others. It becomes "roped off," in a sense, in the child's mind, with a "proceed with caution" sign at the place where it intersects with the rest of the body.

Sensuality

A friend tells a wonderful story about him and his four-year-old son. He was standing in his basement emptying the dryer one morning, when the boy came flying down the stairs as fast as his little legs could manage them. Breathless by the time he reached his father, he could barely get his words out of his mouth.

"DADDY!," he practically shouted as he took a deep breath, "I was just sitting on the toilet! And I was rubbing on my penis! And guess what! It just got bigger and bigger and bigger until it pointed UP TO THE SKY!"

My friend stood there with his mouth aghast and his mind a blank. As the saying goes, he couldn't have thought of something to say at that moment if his life had depended on it. Fortunately for him, he didn't need to say anything. The little boy was gone in a flash, off to explore the next item on his morning's agenda.

As concrete thinkers, young children learn primarily by what they experience directly through their senses. Looking and touching are essential to knowing and understanding, and sexuality is no different. Even infants, once they have developed the requisite motor ability, delight in serendipitously finding and stroking their genitals and in recognizing and enjoying the sensations they can produce. Many continue this fun experiment sporadically throughout the toddler years, especially as diapers are discarded and the genitals are more readily accessible. By age four or five, the behavior may become more frequent and more purposeful, as children discover that rubbing the genitals directly or rubbing them against a handy object is not only pleasurable but a predictable source of soothing relaxation.

For many parents and other caretakers, a young child's fascination with her or his genitals triggers discomfort if not downright upset and concern. Often they are simply embarrassed (we're not exactly used to seeing other people touch their genitals in front of us!), especially if they inappropriately equate the behavior with the much more purposeful, orgasm-driven form of masturbation engaged in by adolescents and adults. Parents might also be worried about the reaction or potential reaction of others who may notice little Jeremy's or Julie's behavior, concerned that these observers, too, might become uncomfortable or might silently judge the child—or the parents—in some negative way because he or she is "touching herself" in public. (What an interesting phrase: Children touch themselves all the time all over their bodies, but everyone knows which particular body parts this phrase automatically connotes!). Parents might also feel very conflicted; they may know or have read or heard that this behavior is "perfectly normal" and that children should not be criticized or punished for it, but they don't know how to put limits around it in public spaces without making the behavior itself seem negative (more on this in Chapter 5).

Most people's discomfort with children's genital touching is also rooted in ignorance and misinformation, as well as guilt or ambivalence regarding their own masturbatory experiences. Long gone are the days (let's hope) when people believed that masturbation causes pimples, blindness, insanity, and hairy palms. But, by the same token, it may be a long time to come before this near-universal behavior loses its enduring stigma and becomes an acceptable and accepted part of the human experience. Given the widespread ignorance about the biology of sexual response—though the reproductive system is immature and totally nonfunctional at birth, the sexual response system is fully functional—it's no wonder that these anxieties are still so frequently projected onto normal childhood behavior.

No matter what the reasons for our discomfort, it's important for parents and other caregivers to examine their attitudes, beliefs, and reactions carefully. Children's earliest experiences with their own eroticism are formative, just like all other important firsts. It will not serve them to be taught that experiencing their bodies as pleasurable is somehow wrong. As researcher and author Elizabeth Roberts points out, "Liking our bodies is part of liking ourselves; what we come to believe about how our bodies should feel, how they should look, and how they should work will exert an important influence on how we perceive and express our sexual selves."

Intimacy

My friend and colleague Bob Selverstone often reads aloud the following passage by Alayn Yates at his sexuality workshops for parents and professionals.

It was dark, the apartment was empty, save for the two of them. As they lay entwined in warm embrace, this room, this bed, was the Universe. Aside from the faint sounds of their tranquil breathing, they were silent. She stroked the nape of his neck. He nuzzled her erect nipple, first gently with his nose, then licked it, tasted it, smelled and absorbed her body odor.

It was a hot and humid August day, and they had been perspiring. Slowly he caressed her one breast as he softly rolled his face over the contours of the other. He pressed his body close against her, sighed, and, fully spent, closed his eyes and soon fell into a deep satisfying sleep.

Ever so slowly she slipped herself out from under him, lest she disturb him, cradled him in her arms and moved him to his crib. Having completed his 6:00 A.M. feeding, the four-month-old had also experienced one more minute contribution to his further sexual development.

"Gotcha!" I said to myself the first time I heard the recitation. It suddenly became clear to me, despite all of my knowledge and training, how deeply conditioned I am to think (and to want to think) of babies as fundamentally asexual and the parent-child bond as purely affectionate. Without hearing the punch line it would never have occurred to me to contemplate this encounter as anything other than lover to lover.

But, of course, mothers and nursing babies *are* "lovers" in many senses of the word. An inseparable "couple," they are enmeshed and absorbed totally in a profoundly close, physically intimate, and mutually dependent relationship, filled with wonder, delight, and immense pleasure. For those of you who have ever fallen in love, does that description sound familiar?

Breast-feeding and other forms of close body contact between parent and infant typically do not produce feelings of sexual arousal. (That they do in some instances just goes to prove that human bodies are easily aroused and that sexual feelings can be completely unintentional and even incidental; I've even heard of women experiencing erotic feelings during childbirth.) However, Yates's description reveals many similarities between infant-parent affection and adult lovemaking. And it also reminds us that sexual relating, at its best, is far more than the manipulation or juxtaposition of a select few body parts but is rather a full mind-and-body (and some would add soul) encounter. Breastfed or not, unless we are severely neglected, all of us first experience this multisensorial, multilevel connection with another human body and being when we are infants; the lucky among us carry the memory and capacity with us into our intimate partnering as adults.

Values

"My wife and I just don't know what to do," the young man starts out. He's waited around quite a while to talk with me after a presentation on childhood sexuality at his child's preschool. "Our four-year-old daughter, Jennie, is obsessed with her mother's breasts. She points and giggles about them all the time and wants to touch them. She makes up funny names for them, which she likes to say in front of company. She's always asking if she can drink her milk from them like the baby does. Worst of all, she even pinches them—sometimes really hard—and even though my wife tells her that it really hurts, she keeps doing it. The pediatrician says she's probably jealous of the baby and just needs more attention from us. We've really tried to do that, but it hasn't helped."

There are many lessons to be learned from this story because there are so many different issues to tackle. My first impulse, as always, was to think the problem through with the father using the five-needs paradigm described in Chapter 1. The pediatrician, of course, was right in her assessment. Jennie was indeed jealous and upset over the intrusion of her new baby sister, and her mother's breasts—and the special, exclusive time that her mom and the baby shared at feeding time—had become the focal point of her anger. Her first need was to be *affirmed,* by her parents' willingness to recognize what a difficult period this had become for her developmentally. Their swift response to the pediatrician's advice was the right and most important step.

My hunch about why Jennie's unpleasant behaviors persisted was that the parents had not recognized or dealt directly with her additional needs for *information, limit setting,* and *values clarification*, and that's what was fueling their predicament. Although Mom had let Jennie know that she was uncomfortable with the pet names and had told her vigorously and repeatedly that the pinching really hurt, the parents had not followed through with any negative consequences or other direct intervention. As a result, they were locked in a power struggle that Jennie was winning; Mom's simply telling Jennie her feelings without acting on them had given Jennie just the "weapon" she needed to get back at her. She was making her mother very unhappy, and she knew it. And, of course, she was also succeeding at getting Mom's attention away from the baby.

The question in my mind was why the parents were so stymied. In talking with the dad it was clear to me that they were skilled parents who in most situations knew how to set limits effectively. What had them stuck in this situation, it became evident, was that this one had to do with a sexual part of Mom's body. "We're afraid we'll stifle her curiosity or make her think that breasts are bad in some way, and we know that wouldn't be healthy for her," he said.

The parents' dilemma was one I hear all the time. Today's parents are very concerned (as well they should be) about instilling healthy sexual attitudes in their children, but at the same time, they themselves are sometimes made so uncomfortable by their own and their children's sexuality that they lose their good common sense in handling situations that—were they nonsexual in nature—would be a piece of cake. "What would you do in any other case where your child was making fun of or physically hurting someone and wouldn't stop after you had corrected her repeatedly?" I asked the father.

"Well, it would definitely call for a 'time out' at least. I'd have to remove her from the situation and tell her she couldn't come back until she changed her behavior," he answered.

"So what stops you from doing that in this situation?" I said.

"Oh," he said. "I get it now."

Yes, it's important for Jennie to feel good about Mom's breasts and about developed breasts in general, especially since one day she'll have her own. But she also needs *clear information* about other concepts as well, like the relationship between sexual body parts and privacy. Mom had used this word with her in articulating her feelings, but wasn't really clear about what it meant. She also hadn't explained how, if breasts were so "private," why she had made hers so accessible to this annoying baby so nonprivately all the time. (That must have been really confusing to Jennie.) She and Dad also needed to *set clear limits* around Jennie's problematic behavior; the message that her conduct was inappropriate and intolerable was not going to stick as long as they continued to tolerate it. Once they understood that it was possible to be sexuality positive *and* to put appropriate and healthy limits around sexuality-related behavior at the same time, the dilemma could be solved.

Finally, what Jennie needed her parents to realize was that by setting limits clearly and firmly, they would also be teaching a lesson about some of the *values* that are most important to them: It's not acceptable to hurt another person, especially if you don't stop when they tell you it hurts; it's not acceptable to make fun of other people's bodies; it's not acceptable to ignore Mom and Dad when they ask you to change your behavior for an important reason. Fundamental values like respect and responsibility are best reinforced through these kinds of teachable moments, and it's never too early to help children understand the connections between those core principles and the issue of sexuality.

Health

Sexual learning is primarily social learning that begins at birth. It goes on all the time everywhere, from birth to death, as we interact with every other sexual and gendered person in our environment. And, in turn, they are learning from us. We are all both students and teachers in this process each and every moment.

Young children, especially, are continually learning about sexuality. Parents, siblings, neighbors, friends, relatives, as well as television, books, and toys are their constant textbooks and mentors. Daily experiences in the family—involving body contact and physical affection; nudity, modesty, genital exploration, and toilet training; curiosity about body parts and functions; gender roles and attitudes toward masculinity and femininity—are children's living laboratories. Ironically, parents are typically unaware of most of the constant sexual learning that is taking place under their tutelage, because they conclude that if nobody is talking or asking about "sex," nothing is being learned about sexuality. Equating sexuality with sexual intercourse in this way dissociates it from the context of life itself and blinds us to its continual presence in our lives and in our children's lives. It causes us to think: There is certainly no sexuality education going on in *this* house. What could a private, grownup act possibly have to do with the lives of infants, toddlers, and young children?

My very first day on the job as a community health educator, in 1971, I attended a training workshop taught by Paul Ephross, a distinguished professor at the University of Maryland School of Social Work. He asked the group to go around the circle and tell a story from our childhood about some sort of "sex education" we had received either at home, in school, or with a peer or sibling. After each person spoke, he asked the same two questions: What exactly did you learn about "sex" in that situation *and*, in addition, what else do think you learned about "sexuality" or about sexual learning?

Interestingly, the participants had a tough time coming up with the exact details of what they had learned (the "sex" part), but they recalled with ease the circumstances that existed around the learning (the "sexuality" part): I learned that people are really embarrassed about this subject. I learned that people like to show off what they know about sex and pretend to know stuff they don't. Boys talk about sex more than girls. I learned (later) that my friends didn't have any idea what they were talking about. I learned my aunt was really easy to talk to and very nonjudgmental. People suddenly lower their voice and get a funny look on their face when they use a sexual term. Adults don't have a clue about what kids really want to know, so kids talk about sex where adults can't hear them. I realize now that, at the time, in the back of my head, I thought to myself, I will *never* ask my mother a question about sex again.

As Albert Einstein once said, education is what remains when everything else you have learned has been forgotten. What Dr. Ephross knew, and what we all came to understand deeply by the end of the session, was that true sexual learning—learning about yourself and others as sexual people—is the part that "sticks," and that's really real, because it's the part that's *experienced*. It's the part that affects how we see ourselves and other people, how we think, how we feel, what we value, how we relate, how we communicate, and how we make decisions.

The life of very young children is all about experience. The fact that most adults are unaware of the sexual levels of those experiences means that they cannot be as thoughtful and proactive as they might about setting up what educator Elizabeth Roberts calls the proper "conditions of sexual learning." Those crucial conditions of learning will determine much about our children's future sexual health and well-being—intellectually, physically, socially, emotionally, and spiritually. They will help shape their capacity for physical and emotional intimacy and their enjoyment of physical affection and erotic pleasure; the extent to which they come to see their bodies as a source of pride, delight, and self-knowledge; their understanding of what it means to be a boy or girl, man or woman; the ease with which they incorporate and use sexual information and knowledge and communicate their sexual needs and feelings; their capacity for empathy, and the ability to think carefully about sexual values and morality.

As we become more and more aware of the conditions of sexual learning in our children's lives, we will become better parents and teachers, and a more healthy, positive, and nurturing society. And, most important, we will have enhanced the capacity of children everywhere to make more informed, responsible, and satisfying decisions for the rest of their lives.

3

Where Did I Come From?

In Chapter 2, we explored the notion of sexual learning as a rich and multifaceted enterprise, residing in the young child's dynamic experience of living, growing, and interacting. Please keep in mind, though, that this emphasis on indirect learning is not meant at all to detract from the significance of direct verbal communication in a child's life: What we tell (or don't tell) our children about sexuality and *how* we tell it also have lasting implications.

Misplaced Anxieties

In my work, I'm continually amazed at how we adults tend to attach such huge intrinsic power to sexual information—to the extent that its supposed impact on children has become distorted far beyond what is even faintly reasonable. Far from "protecting" our children, this misappropriated anxiety only short-circuits our thinking about their real developmental needs and causes much unnecessary second-guessing and hand-wringing about the issue of "age appropriate-ness." As the saying goes, if I had a nickel for every time a parent has asked me "But are you *sure* it's really okay for my child to know _____ at his age?," I'd be ready to retire.

When I first became a sexuality educator in the early 1970s, many adults were genuinely frightened of providing sexual infor-mation to young people even when they were in high school. Parents relaxed to a degree only during their children's mid- to late teen years, often by convincing themselves, "Oh well, I guess they already know about it anyway." It was as if there was some magical time when it was "just right" and then—and only then—was it okay for them to know about sex. (The other presumption, of course, was that, unless adults decided to tell you about sex, you couldn't and wouldn't find out about it elsewhere.) The problem was, it wasn't at all clear just when a young person was actually supposed to be "old enough." If only there was a gizmo of some sort that you could buy in a store (or the pediatrician's office), like a meat thermometer, that you could use to divine irrefutably when the timing was "just right."

Since the exact moment of readiness was undetermined, it was prudent simply to wait as long as possible. But in many families, as the years went by, waiting to tell became in effect not telling at all. Many people even today remember with nostalgia and amusement the awkward talks their mother or father attempted to have with them on the eve of their wedding day.

Most children in the United States now receive some kind of sex education both in middle and high school, and some form of "puberty education" in late elementary school. As a legacy from the past, however, many programs below high school are astoundingly behind where they could and should be in terms of what children and adolescents are capable of understanding. Imagine if someone arbitrarily were to decide that arithmetic wasn't appropriate to teach until fifth grade and that long division should be put off until ninth. And then, imagine that everyone else—parents, teachers, administrators, and school board members—reacted to this conclusion by saying, "Oh, okay. That sounds about right." In many parts of the country, that's pretty much the process, or lack of process, used to determine what is and isn't taught about sexuality.

Truthfully, the current state of affairs nationally is the direct result much more often of political expediency than of any other factor. (School systems don't like controversy, and those individuals and groups opposed to comprehensive sexuality education in schools are sure to initiate it if programs become too broad in focus.) Moreover, in many school districts, some of the information that almost everyone agrees *could* be taught at certain ages from a pedagogical perspective is deliberately *not* taught as a matter of principle—not because it is considered *age* inappropriate but because it is considered *morally* inappropriate (commonly, information about condoms, contraception, abortion, and homosexuality, for example). But, it is also certainly true that, politics aside, *enormous* ignorance still exists in the educational community and in society at large about what kind of sexual information is appropriate to teach children and at what ages.

Listen First, Lesson Plan Later

In line with what I've said about the 1970s, when I first began teaching courses in human sexuality it was to high-school juniors and seniors. Gradually over several years, the program was expanded to include earlier and earlier grade levels, as more attention was focused on the needs of younger children and adolescents. In part this extension occurred in response to feedback from older students that the information and concepts provided to them, although helpful, were woefully "too little, too late."

Year after year, as I've taken on more and more grade levels (I now teach every grade from fourth through twelfth), I've found myself in the same novice position. Never having taught each year's new grade or grades before, I was at a loss once again to know what was "age appropriate" for this new batch of kids—other than what I could intuit by having observed the knowledge, questions, needs, interests, gaps, misunderstandings, and confusions evident among the previous batch of slightly older kids the year before.

So, year by year, what I learned to do was to keep a simple rule: Listen first and lesson plan later. This rule, I've learned, is the only surefire and true yardstick for measuring what children should, can, and need to know about sexuality at *any age*. We adults don't need a gizmo, I've decided. We just need to be willing to listen and to trust our children and our students to know and tell us what they need.

Following Our Children's Lead

Like me, you as a parent are a novice teacher asked to teach a new "grade level" every year. My advice to you is the same I've always given myself, to listen first and lesson plan later.

If we listen very carefully even to the youngest of our children, they'll tell us not only *what* they want to know but also *how they think* about what they want to know and *why* they're thinking about it in the first place.

First Questions, First Clues

Often I advise parents who are struggling mightily with the issue of age appropriateness in relation to their elementary- and middle-school–aged children to think about the following questions: "Let's try to look at a bigger context here in order to gain some perspective. At what age, in your own recollection, do very young children spontaneously begin to ask the kinds of questions that will lead—if we follow—to a discussion of topics like sex and reproduction? And, what is the first question they are likely to ask?"

The youngest age I usually hear mentioned—and also the most common—is four years. And the question? "Where do babies come from?" or its more personalized version, "Where did *I* come from?"

"What's the next question and the next age likely to be," I ask them, "and the next?"

Almost universally I am told "How did I get out of there?" (age five), followed by "How did I get in there *in the first place*?" (age six).

Although there may be some slight discrepancies regarding order and timing, most parents, upon hearing others identify this sequence—this trilogy—of early childhood questions nod comfortably and look at each other in knowing agreement.

Noticing this consistency in what parents had to say over many years, I became a great admirer of the work of Anne Bernstein, best known for her important book *The Flight of the Stork: What Children Think (and When) About Sex and Family Building*. As part of her research in the late 1970s at the University of California at Berkeley, Bernstein interviewed dozens of children between the ages of three and twelve about their understandings of "where babies come from." She gave no information whatsoever to the children during the interviews, just simply asked questions like: How do people get babies? How do mommies become mommies? How did your dad get to be a dad?

What she discovered was remarkable. Regardless of any prior information about reproduction children had been told or not told—and despite their often humorous, contradictory, and highly personalized versions of the various events in the process—children at like ages and stages of development displayed striking similarities in the *ways* they thought and theorized about creation. From her data, she identified six different *levels of thought*, spanning the spectrum from ages three to twelve, which corresponded neatly to the general stages of cognitive development classified earlier by the esteemed Swiss psychologist Jean Piaget.

It was her "level one" classification, "Geography," that really got me thinking about what I had been hearing parents say about the same issue, only coming at it from a slightly different perspective. To Bernstein's ear, level-one children (usually three to four years old) answered the question "How do people get babies?" as if it were a question about geography. They would say things like: "You go to the store and buy one." "They come from God's place." "They grow in mommies' tummies." Asked where babies were before they were in each of these places, the children would simply name another place that seemed logical to them at the moment (for example, some other mommy's tummy).

Children who are reasoning at the level-one stage have no understanding of the laws of cause and effect. Their belief that babies have always existed is consistent with their limited intellectual understanding of the concepts of time, space, and distance. At this stage they are simply incapable of imagining a world in which they and all of the other people they know do not exist; they are able to reason only within the limited framework of their particular level of understanding and no further.

Where Did I Come From?

Just as Bernstein came to appreciate how children understand the process of reproduction by eliciting their answers, so you can come to the same understanding by carefully listening to your child's questions.

When children first spring the "where did I come from?" question, parents commonly make the mistake of leaping way ahead of the level at which the question is being asked. "Uh-oh," you may think, "she wants to know about SEX!"

There are a couple of good reasons why we do this. First, as adults we have long been capable of, and are very used to, reasoning about this and other issues quite facilely at what Bernstein refers to as level-six thinking, the level of "Physical Causality." *We* know very well that sex—really sexual intercourse—is the mechanism through which babies come into being (in most cases). We simply forget to remember that children's thinking operates at a very different level, and we mistakenly project our more complex thought process onto theirs.

Or perhaps it isn't quite so simple after all. If a four-year-old child were to ask what makes the car go, we would probably realize in a heartbeat that a perfectly adequate answer would not require a detailed explanation of carburetors, fuel pumps, and engine cylinders. Almost instinctively, we would know to say, "You step on the gas pedal," or something along those lines, and that would be that. That's because we don't carry around a trunk load of baggage about cars and how they locomote. Conversations about sex (or ones we *think* are about sex) usually cause a great deal more unnecessary confusion and consternation. Our mishaps are a classic example of how our anxiety about *this topic* can cause us so quickly to lose our good common sense.

Here's the point: When a four-year-old asks, "Where did I come from?" he means just that. Literally, *where* did I come from. That is, *where* as in *geographically* where. He or she is not talking or asking about sex at all, doesn't know about it, doesn't feel a need to know about it, and therefore hasn't a whit of interest in it. Rather, this is a question that has just occurred to him about his previous address or whereabouts. His brain has only just now matured to a stage where he can suddenly understand that he wasn't always *here*. He'd simply like to know where it is that he *used* to be.

All that guesswork that my parents' generation went through to try and determine how to detect the exact moment of "readiness" for this information or that information, when it was right there in front of them all the time! Discerning what children need and want to know about sexuality and reproduction is often just this simple.

Another way of understanding why children's questions about their origins commonly surface at about age four has to do with the child's developing understanding of herself and others as separate beings, and of the physical world as made up of finite objects. Whereas as infants and toddlers their assumption was "I am the universe and the universe is me," three- and four-year-olds have learned and accepted that they—and all other people and objects—have a clear beginning and ending *in space*. This insight parallels their growing understanding that people and things also have a clear beginning and ending *in time*. (It's no coincidence that it's also at about age four when children begin to talk about and ask questions about death.) Children at this age also can understand and accept for the first time why they are not present in certain family pictures taken before they were born. Just as "Where did I come from?" is shorthand for "Where was I before I was here?" it's also a paraphrase of the thought "Since I've just had the realization that everything in life has a clear beginning and ending, I'm thinking that I must have had a beginning, too. Please tell me, where was my beginning?"

As for "How did I get out of there?" and "How did I get in there in the first place?," as we'll see, those questions aren't really questions about SEX! either, but about the child's desire to know more about himself and his "place" in his ever-enlarging physical and intellectual world.

How Did I Get out of There?

In her delightful and insightful book *Your Child at Play: Three to Five Years*, Marilyn Segal offers a marvelous window into how preschool children think about time—the concept that will beget, so to speak, their next questions about origins.

Like faraway places, Segal says, the concept of time for three- to five-year-olds is very mysterious. Where is yesterday? they want to know. Will it ever be tomorrow? How long before it's later? What happened to now? Where do you keep the time that you "save"?

Although time stretches out in both a forward and backward direction, Segal points out that a young child's understanding of how time extends into the past and the future is asymmetrical. Because she has memories of the past that are stored in her mind—and which can be recalled at will in her thoughts and recounted vividly in conversation—the past has a "tangible" quality that makes it easier for her to think about and understand. Having *experienced* the past or, more accurately, having had *experiences in* the past, the past is more concrete and therefore "real" than the total abstraction called "future."

Tuned-in parents and teachers can actually take a step back and watch their preschoolers as they incrementally develop greater and greater levels of sophistication in thinking about the past and, eventually, the future. A child may suddenly say, for example, "We haven't seen Grandma in a long while." Or, one afternoon, he may come home and without prodding begin to recite the entire string of events that occurred during the school day or at a birthday party or some other special event, one-by-one, in perfectly correct order. And, once children become more facile at organizing their past intellectually, the present and the future will also become easier for them to understand and to manipulate in language and thought. New words and concepts—like before, now, later; yesterday, today, tomorrow; next, soon, a while, and sometime; Monday and Tuesday, weekdays and weekends—begin to have real meaning.

As Segal points out, one clue that children have begun to think with greater ease about the concept of future is their expanding ability to understand the timetable marking their own growth and development. They will begin to divide their future life span into general age categories—big children, teenagers, and grownups— and they'll start to identify certain milestones that punctuate the beginnings and endings of each stage. They'll work hard at understanding the relationships among immediate and extended family members, like who was born first and last and who was born to whom. All of these new pieces of information will gradually become woven together and integrated into their overall mastery of the concept of time, and at the same time heighten their growing interest in baby and family making.

Beside the concept of *growth over time*, another theme ever present in the minds of four- to six-year-olds involves *movement over time.* Five-year-olds, especially, seem to love learning about locomotion and transportation in all of their various forms— sometimes, as you may well have noticed, to the point of obses- sion. No doubt, their fascination with this special kind of move- ment results from its appeal to the senses—they not only love to watch vehicles move and to watch *from* vehicles that *are* moving, they enjoy the *feel and sound* of the movement itself. However, they are also beginning intellectually to grasp the purposeful and utilitarian aspects of movement, as a means of getting from here to there.

Perhaps you have figured out where I am heading with all of this seemingly extraneous "stuff" about time and movement. At some point, at about age five, all of these new understandings about time, distance, and movement and about the temporal and physi- cal relationships that exist among family members will suddenly coalesce in the child's mind, and a new set of questions about his or her origins will form: "How interesting. I just thought of some- thing! A while back, Dad (or Mom, or Grandpa, or my teacher) told me that before I was here, I used to be in Mom's uterus. Well, if *before* I was in there, and *now* I'm out here, how did that happen? I wonder, how did I get *from in there to out here!*"

So, as with the "where did I come from" question, the child's seeming interest in SEX!—about which she or he still doesn't know anything, doesn't feel a need to know anything, and therefore isn't interested in one whit—is really about the issues of *time and place* and, in this case, their close conceptual cousins, *distance and movement.*

In short, while the child previously, for quite some time, was intellectually satisfied with an explanation of his origins that relied on an understanding of *geography* and *beginnings and endings,* he now (and only now) understands that there are other important features of the story to consider: *distance and transportation.* His new question, "How did I get out of there?" is perfectly timed and matched, therefore, to this new level of intellectual sophistication and thematic interest. And as we'll see, this new theme will guide us handily in figuring out how best to answer.

The Big One: But How Did I
Get in There in the First Place?

Again, let's start by painting a larger developmental picture.

At age six most children are ready—emotionally, socially, and intellectually—for "real" school. By this time, most children undergo a major transition in the way they think about and approach the world, a change that can make the cognitive differences between five- and six-year-olds quite dramatic. The six-year-old begins to understand the world—and increasingly *wants* to understand it—from a point of view that is decidedly more adultlike in approach. Many shifts occur in the child's logic and reasoning abilities that make these new ways of thinking possible (changes which Jean Piaget recognized as the beginning of what he called "operational thought").

Two of these shifts in mental capacity in particular help explain why children's questions about their origins at this age often take a huge leap forward in intellectual sophistication. One shift is marked by the child's ability to reverse an idea through mental activity, and the second by an increasing understanding and ability to apply the concept of cause and effect as it occurs in the natural world.

The process of "thinking in reverse" means a child can logically follow the course of an event from beginning to end and then make an intellectual U-turn in his own mind and follow the steps in reverse order back to the very first one. Here's an example from one of Piaget's classic experiments: Two equal balls of clay are placed in front of the child. One is rolled out into a clay "snake" and the child is asked to compare the amount of clay in both objects.

Whereas a five-year-old typically will see the snake as containing "more" clay than the ball because it is longer, a six-year-old will know they are equal in quantity. She can mentally reverse the activity of unrolling the ball in her mind and then keep it there, even while she is looking at two distinctly different-looking objects.

By age six, children begin to understand that everything in nature follows a consistent pattern of logic: Cause A will lead to effect B, all the time and in every circumstance (unless something happens to intervene), because that is how the laws of nature work. Gravity *always* works to pull objects downward (unless you're in a space capsule); the sky is blue *because* light is reflected a certain way; the sun goes away and comes back as the world turns on its axis. The child's logic at this age is certainly not perfect and is often simplistic—one six-year-old I know whose grandmother died of complications from a massive heart attack searched angrily for an explanation and decided that, since she was well the day before she went into the hospital but died four days later, it was the experience of being in the hospital itself that had killed her—but the child understands deeply, nonetheless, that *everything* that happens does have a cause.

So one day, as the child is practicing these new and interesting ways of reasoning, he is reminded in some way about the topic of his origins. He thinks about the fact that he used to be in Mom's uterus, and he remembers your explanation of how he came out. Then he reverses his own mental image. He pictures himself back in the womb. He knows that he was there, but for the first time he begins to wonder how he might have gotten there to begin with. Suddenly, a thought occurs to him: Hey, if everything in the world has a cause, then I must have had a cause, too! I wonder, how was I made? How was *I* caused? *How did I come to be in Mom's uterus in the first place?*

The child, his mind now firmly and comfortably at home in Bernstein's "Manufacturing" stage, is capable of understanding that babies (and he) have not always existed and must somehow be "built"; our young philosopher continues the work of making his universe intelligible on brand new levels.

Okay, So I've Got the Questions Down: Now What?

In Chapter 1, we acknowledged that for many of us, "Caution! Proceed very carefully, if at all!" was the prevailing rule about sexual learning when we were growing up. To keep us "safe," parents and other adults attempted to keep the topics of sex and reproduction hidden and apart from the rest of life. When we ourselves become parents, even at a very different time and age, that same "protective" mantra may resurface unexpectedly, encouraging us to recreate the same artificial divide. Unless we have an opportunity to challenge these old family "tapes," we may end up perpetuating the mistaken belief that sexuality is "different" and must be treated differently than other subjects about which children are so naturally curious.

This same unnecessary divide can create a paralyzing disconnect within ourselves between the subject of sexuality and all of the helpful things we know so easily and well about dealing with the rest of life—as in the case of the father mentioned in Chapter 2, distraught over his daughter Jennie's "breast obsession." Once he discovered that his dilemma wasn't really about SEX! at all but about one of the central developmental issues of living with a four-year-old, called *limit setting*, he knew immediately what he needed to do. His good common sense finally snapped back into place, like the last piece of a jigsaw puzzle that's been lost under the living room sofa for years.

The fact that young children's questions about their origins, as well, are not really about sex at all but about generic intellectual constructs—place, time, distance, movement, and causation—can also be enormously reassuring to parents and other caretakers. I love to watch the faces of participants in my workshops when they "get it." Such relief!—not so much because they immediately stop worrying about what they might have perceived as an abnormal interest in "sex" on their children's part as because they suddenly know that they can do this job now (it's gone from daunting to doable). And, though children's interest in their origins is not directly about sex—at least at the start (it does end up there)—part of what parents "get" is that they'll be able to handle that discussion too. They understand now how and why the whole story can, should, and eventually will come out.

In other words, you and your children have been successfully studying topics like space, time, distance, movement, and causation together for years. All you need to do now is help them apply what they've already discovered about these very same principles to a new topic, the study of reproduction.

Although you as a parent will come up with your own natural way of saying and explaining things, the best approach, generally, is the following: Take the child's lead, offer a relatively short, direct, and simple (but accurate!) answer, and then stop and see what happens next. Also, as we said earlier, another important tip is to remember to interpret the child's question as literally as possible. (Expect some missteps on your part along the way; they're probably inevitable.)

So, if the question is "*Where* did I come from?," answer by naming a *place:* "You're wondering where you were before you were born. All children wonder about that sooner or later. Before you were born you were in a special place or organ inside mom's body called her uterus (or womb) that kept you safe so you could live and grow until you were ready to come out."

For the "transportation" question, "How did I get out of there?," parents can say something like: "What a good question! It really makes sense that you would be wondering how you could have gotten from a place *inside* Mommy's belly to the space *outside* her body. Well, right next to mom's uterus—remember, that's the place where you grew for nine months before you were born—there's another special organ called a vagina. The vagina is a connecting place between the uterus and the outside, and it has an opening between Mom's legs. When you were ready to be born, mom's uterus pushed really hard (it works like a muscle) and after a while it pushed you through the vagina until you came through the opening. And that's how you came out!" (Since the child will have difficulty visualizing things she or he cannot see directly, having some books handy with clear diagrams will be very helpful.)

The "causation" question can be handled in just the same matter-of-fact manner but will very likely require a longer conversation or perhaps even a series of talks over several weeks or months—not because it's about SEX!, but because the processes involved are even more invisible and the steps are more complex.

> *Step 1:* "Here's how you were made. Inside Dad's body there are tiny little objects—so small you can't see them with your eye—called sperm. They are located in his testicles, which are two ball-shaped organs that are inside a sac right behind the penis. Inside Mom's body, near her uterus, there are different tiny cells called egg cells or ova that are kept in a place called ovaries. When a sperm from a man comes together with an egg from a woman, that's called fertilization, and that's how babies are started." This is a lot of new information all at once for many children; the parent could start with the simple statement "You were made by two small cells called a sperm and an ova" and fill in the rest of the information as the child continues to ask questions like "What is a sperm? Where does it come from?" Or the parent could take the other route and start with "Daddy and I made you together" or "You were made by parts of me and Mom."

Step 2: Sooner or later, the child will say something like "But I don't understand. If sperm are kept *inside* Dad's body, and eggs are kept *inside* Mom's body, then how can they get together?" "What a great question!" you could respond. "You have just put your finger on a very interesting design problem that nature (or God, as you might prefer to say) had to figure out how to solve. In order for the sperm and egg to be able to join, nature designed male and female bodies to be able to fit together like puzzle pieces. When the bodies are fit together, the sperm and egg can find one another."

Step 3: You probably know what's coming next: "But how *exactly* do they do that?" "You know that Dad has a penis and Mom has a vagina, right? Well, remember we talked about the fact that vaginas are connected on the inside of Mom's body to the uterus and on the outside of Mom's body to an opening between her legs? Like all other body openings, things can come out of vaginas, but things can go in, too.

"When a man and a woman make a baby, the man's penis becomes bigger and stiffer. When that happens, we say his penis is having an erection, and when a penis is erect, it is just the size and shape it needs to be so it can fit right into the vagina. When the penis and vagina are joined in this way (just like puzzle pieces!), that's called sexual intercourse.

"While intercourse is happening, sperm come out of the end of the penis and swim (sperm look and act like teeny little tadpoles) farther inside the woman's body where one of them can meet an egg. As we said before, when the sperm and egg come together, that's called fertilization. Once fertilization happens, the egg will travel to the uterus where it will grow for the next nine months until it is ready to come out of the mom's vagina.

"So now you have the whole story because we're right back to the place we started from when you asked, 'Where did I come from?' Now you know the whole story—where you came from, how you got out, and how you got in there in the first place!"

Not "Whew!" but "Wow!"

For many parents, the idea of having to explain the process of reproduction is something they dread. Isn't that a shame! The twin miracles of giving our children life and of bringing children into our lives are, for most of us, among the most joyous and meaningful events in our entire lives. Why should the experience of sharing about those events with our children be any less joyous or meaningful? Our reaction, or theirs, shouldn't have to be, "Whew, we finally got that one over with!" It should be, "WOW! Wasn't that neat, and fun, and amazing!"

How wonderful for us, and for our children, if that's a goal we know we can all aim for.

4

Parents Have Questions, Too!

By far the most common questions that parents of young children ask have to do with explaining the concept of origins. They often have many other questions and issues on their mind, however, *around* the process of teaching, learning, and communicating. You'll probably find some of your own in the following examples.

Suppose My Child Doesn't Ask or Doesn't Ask in This Way?

Because so many parents have told me, I know that understanding the trilogy of questions and answers presented in Chapter 3 can be enormously helpful and that the questions and sequences that I've observed closely fit the patterns experienced in many families.

I often worry, however, that by laying out this timetable and sequence as I have, I risk creating new problems and pressures for parents by inadvertently encouraging you to assume that this is the way the process *always* goes or *should*. Therefore, you may think, should your family's experience deviate in some way, it must mean there is something wrong in either your child's pace of development or your own parenting.

Nothing could be further from the truth. Every child is different and grows according to his or her own unique, innate timetable of developmental change. Some children ask these or similar questions earlier than I've indicated, some later. Many save them up and ask them all at once or in a different order. Some children never ask them at all. All of these children and all of these patterns are "normal."

Rather than setting up hard-and-fast expectations, the points that I'm really hoping to make are the following: (1) We should not be at all surprised if children as young as four, five, and six ask these kinds of questions about their origins; (2) we should not ever be afraid to answer a young child's questions on the levels at which they are being asked, and we should listen carefully to ascertain those levels; and (3) since sexuality is a part of life, questions about sexuality are simply part of a child's ongoing repertoire of *life questions* that he is constantly asking himself—and adults—as he attempts to make meaning of his world. Only because we are trained to think otherwise do we hear their questions as being about SEX!

Does a Four- (or Five- or Six-) Year-Old Really Need to Know This Stuff?

The answer to this question is a definitive "no" and an equally definitive "yes."

As I've said, many children at these ages have yet to ask about their origins; it hasn't crossed their mind just yet, and/or they may not have been exposed to things in their environment to help stimulate their thinking. And there are parents who choose to avoid or put off these kinds of questions indefinitely either because they're too uncomfortable or because they truly believe their children really are "too young." This is no great tragedy—all of these children can and probably will grow up just fine!

That said, my bias must be obvious by now. Hearing this question always makes me want to ask: Is it okay for a four- (or five- or six-) year-old to know about geography, or transportation, or causation (because that's what questions about origins are really about)? Does she or he really *need* to know about *these* things? Well, certainly not absolutely, but having that kind of knowledge unquestionably will help her or his future learning capacity. And, *not* knowing may certainly hamper or slow it down considerably, since learning—for young children especially—occurs in an ever lengthening spiral formation. I think that, at the very least, we'd have to acknowledge that having this knowledge certainly couldn't hurt.

I think this last point may be at the bottom of what prompts the question in the first place. The "really need to know this" part of the question intimates to me at least a tinge of negativity—either about the subject of sexuality itself or about sexual learning—and the belief that maybe knowing this information really *could* hurt. And that's an attitude, as I've said, I'd encourage all parents to examine very carefully.

Finally, in today's world especially, there are many other competing sources of information, attitudes, and values about sexuality to which children are exposed (and at younger and younger ages), with peers and media among the most important and ever present. Apart from and even more important than any particular facts parents may impart, those who invite and encourage their young children's curiosity about sexuality also teach a loud and clear message about themselves as parents: I am available—and I always will be—as an accepting and authoritative resource on these and all other matters you may want to know about. Conversely, parents who distance themselves from these kinds of conversations inadvertently may undermine their credibility as available, reliable resources.

What Other Kinds of Questions Can I Expect to Be Asked?

Everyone who spends any time at all with young children can't help but be charmed and astonished by the wonderful questions they pose. Because they view the world with fresh eyes and because they are changing so rapidly, every day brings new ways of seeing and thinking about all of the myriad things and experiences that, most often, adults have been taking for granted for years.

Even we adults, of course, are awed and captivated by the miracle of creation, so one can only imagine a young child's level of curiosity and excitement. Once the topic is opened up, parents can expect many, many questions about growing babies and about the processes of labor and birth: How does the baby grow? How does it fit in the mother's tummy? How does it get to be a he or a she? How does it eat? Does it sleep, and how does it go to the bathroom? When the mother eats or drinks, does the baby get wet or hit in the face? What does the baby do in there all day? What does it do when the mother is asleep? Will it like me? Can it hear me? Can I play with it when it comes out? Is there ever a baby in the daddy's tummy? When will there be a baby in my tummy? How does the baby get out of such a small opening? Does it hurt the mom? Does it hurt the baby? How come the baby doesn't fall out before it's ready? Were you there when I was born? Did I cry when I came out? Could you put the new baby back in (please!) after it's born?

Some questions will be easy to answer, and others not so easy often because they involve processes that are either complex or very difficult to visualize. You'll find that diagrams will be very helpful, as well as analogies; turtlenecks, for example, come in very handy for explaining how a baby's head can come out of such a relatively small opening. Sometimes questions are challenging because we're afraid the answers might be upsetting or frightening. The best rule of thumb in that case is to always give truthful information but in a balanced way: "Yes, it hurts sometimes when you give birth, but the mother can take medicine to help her feel much better." Expect, too, to hear some of the same questions over and over, since it's hard for the children to hold on to concepts that are not entirely concrete. Thankfully, any topic that is too far beyond their intellectual reach will quickly become boring, and something else will catch their interest and attention before too long.

Should you be expecting, you'll soon become a veritable walking, talking visual aid. Children will enjoy watching your abdomen grow and delight in feeling the baby's movements. (My older son watched hypnotically one day as his baby brother's hiccuping caused my bulging belly to pop out rhythmically every few seconds for twenty minutes straight!) As the pregnancy advances and as their knowledge grows, they'll often spend hours acting out the whole process. One little girl I heard about would line up all of her stuffed animals in a row every morning, listen attentively to their abdomens with her play stethoscope, and give each a detailed status report on the progress of his or her "pregnancy." Many children (girls and boys) will put dolls or other objects under their clothing and pretend to give birth. As the delivery date approaches, their play will often intensify as they attempt to work through their escalating feelings of excitement, tension, or anxiety. I still have the drawings my son created in the weeks leading up to his brother's birth. For days he sketched nothing but boxes inside of boxes, always with an arrow at the very center pointing outward. Once the delivery was over, he immediately began to draw colorful pictures of open skies and fields.

One cautionary note: In many families, for obvious reasons of timing, a child's first questions about origins are likely to coincide with the pregnancy or birth of a younger sibling—prompting everyone to assume, quite logically, that one event has precipitated the other. However, that is not entirely the case, and we should not be misled. It is vital to understand that, for the most part, questions about origins are generated *internally* in tandem with the child's evolving cognitive abilities, not *externally* because of some dramatic precipitating event. When children are ready, they will ask about their origins in the total absence of pregnant women or newborns, and when they're not, mom could be expecting triplets and it won't really matter.

What About My (or My Child's) Embarrassment?

Embarrassment, yours and/or your child's, is something you can expect to surface during conversations about sexuality from time to time. It will show up in various forms—giggling, joking around, fidgeting, tenseness, avoidance, diverted eyes, lowered voices, silence, and of course, that universal embarrassment giveaway, blushing. The key to handling embarrassment connected to talking about sex is to deal with the feelings very directly and to understand and remember how this kind of embarrassment differs from what I'll call "normal" or "natural" embarrassment.

Everyone knows all too well the experience of saying or doing something we think is really lame or idiotic in front of a bunch of other people and, upon realizing it, wanting desperately to die or disappear on the spot. (How cruel of nature to make us blush unfailingly under these very circumstances and thereby look even more obvious and ridiculous!) This is what I mean by normal, natural embarrassment, and our very human capacity for it—alas—will never go away.

Embarrassment connected with talking about sex is not "normal" and "natural" in the same way at all, because it is totally a *learned* response left over from our experiences and associations during childhood. Therefore, over time and with new experiences, it can be *unlearned*. With practice (most sex educators, present company included, will admit that when they first started to teach they spent many self-conscious moments in front of the mirror repeating certain words over and over until they could finally say them comfortably) the formerly automatic association between embarrassment and conversing about sex will begin to dissipate. I once heard the very wise advice that, when their babies are very young and can't possibly understand, parents should deliberately carry on one-sided conversations with them using the correct terms for sexual anatomy and physiology as if they were common everyday terms. By the time the infant becomes ready to acquire language, teaching the names for her or his body parts and functions will be comfortably second nature.

Remember that the goal of becoming more comfortable is being able to communicate your relaxed, matter-of-fact attitude to your child. In childhood and early adolescence, embarrassment about sexuality most commonly manifests itself in giggles, laughter, silliness, and joke making, behaviors that make it look as if sex is not a subject that is or should be taken seriously. The message adults need to communicate and reinforce is *just the opposite one*—that sexuality is a fundamentally serious subject and that it's appropriate, therefore, to act, look, and sound fundamentally serious when we speak about it. Encourage your child to verbalize his or her feelings instead of acting them out indirectly, especially through nervous laughter. If you try to talk over your embarrassment—or your child's—and don't deal with it directly, she or he will likely remain stuck with it as a learned association, and an unnecessary learning and communication barrier.

Don't misunderstand—laughing and enjoying yourselves during conversations about sex is perfectly okay as long as the fun is about something really funny. When one of my sons was in preschool, he picked up lots of silly terms for penises from other children in his class. At home he'd run through the litany of names at least once a day, laughing and giggling hysterically. Finally I'd had enough of this thoroughly boring and annoying game and told him so. "Penises are a part of your body, and your body is something to be taken seriously," I said. "Besides, penises are really neat organs and they can do all kinds of really neat things." I challenged him to name all the things he knew about penises, and we spent several minutes talking about this unusually versatile body part. (Part of me was saying to myself at the time, I can't *believe* I'm actually having this conversation!) When we couldn't think of anything else to say—by this time, his tone was totally attentive and respectful, almost to the point of awe—I asked, "And what do you think you learned about penises today?" "Well," he said in his most serious and grown up voice, "I learned that penises are fun but not funny!" We both laughed (because that was really funny). That about summed it all up nicely, I thought.

Suppose I Don't Feel Prepared to Answer, or It's the Wrong Time or Place?

One of my very favorite books on sexuality education is the classic *What to Say After You Clear Your Throat* by Jean Gochros. It stays on the parenting book list I give out at my workshops, even though it's long out of print, because the title always makes parents laugh out loud (and at themselves) and reminds them of the collective boat we're all in when it comes to talking to our children about sensitive and complicated subjects.

Children often ask questions about sex or reproduction at the most unexpected or inconvenient times. (Of course, the feeling of inconvenience is always on our end; from the child's perspective, there's never any time like the present for receiving an answer to an utterly fascinating question one has just formulated.) Gesturing to the tampon dispenser, they'll wonder out loud, and loudly, "What's that?" just because we happen to be standing in line in a very crowded public bathroom. They'll point to a pregnant woman's belly in the department store and ask, "Did that baby grow from its mom's egg and dad's sperm like I did?" They'll want to know "Are you and Dad planning on having sex any time soon?" when you're trying to keep your eyes on a very crowded road (that one's a story from my own family archives!).

Here's an important rule of thumb: Answering a young child's question about sex or reproduction is rarely an emergency, and a *good response* is not always a *specific answer* to a specific question. You can always say something like: "That's a great question but I really can't concentrate right now, so we'll talk about it later," or "You know, I'm not quite sure how to explain that topic to someone your age, so give me a little while and I'll explain it to you later." And, if the child is old enough to understand the concept of privacy, it's always appropriate to say, "Remember when I said some things are best for us to talk about when we're alone, just the two of us? Well, this is one of those topics, so let's wait until we get home, okay?" (Or, alternatively, you could say to yourself, "What's *really* so wrong with answering a question like that in a place like this?" and simply answer the question!) Remember, too, that your child, as always, will be paying close attention to your nonverbal communication—voice tone, body language, facial expressions, and the like—no matter what you may choose to say in response to her or his questions. It's best to try to remain calm and shockproof whenever possible, which you'll be better able to do if you remember to always expect the unexpected!

By the way, be forewarned, as many seasoned parents will tell you, that the car is actually a frequent locale for sex education questions of all kinds, and for all kinds of good reasons. First, everyone is a captive audience and there's no easy escape; it's also for many families prime quality time because there's a feeling of togetherness and because everyone's only doing two things at once: sitting or driving and talking. (In most families the pace outside the car is much more frenetic most of the time). And for the shy or embarrassed, there's little or no opportunity for eye contact (especially if it's dark!), and there may be the added comfort and distance of being in the back seat or the wayback. (By the way, parents of teenagers are often the

ones to use the car as a prime location for bringing up sensitive questions or issues, for many of the same reasons!)

Who Should Do the Talking?

The stereotypical image of the "big talk"—with the obligatory
sweaty palms and throat clearing—is a far cry from the fun, easy-
going, everyday conversations that make for healthy family communication about sexuality. It will help if you remember to stay
calm, trust in the process, and welcome your children's questions—
all of them—as unique and precious opportunities.

Parents often ask if it's better for the same-gender parent to do
most of the talking to an individual child. Certainly there are some
instances when that approach might be a good one, depending on
the topic and circumstance, but as a general rule there is no reason
why mothers or fathers should restrict themselves to particular
topics (or offspring). In any case, what kids need most is to witness
as many different kinds of combinations of people speaking openly and respectfully about sexuality as possible—men talking to
women, women to women, men to men, women to boys, men to
girls, boys to girls, girls to girls, boys to boys—so that conversations of all kinds become normalized.

How Much Is *Too* Much?

The near obsession in American culture with the issue of *quantity* of sexual *knowledge* versus *quality* of sexual *communication* is
a topic we've addressed in earlier chapters. It's high time we put
the "too much too soon" myth and its corollary, the belief that
sexual knowledge is somehow *inherently* dangerous, to rest for
good.

That said, imparting information about sex and reproduction to
young children can be tricky because of its inherently complicated

nature. Here are some helpful tips to remember that will help the process go more easily.

Stay Concrete in Your Explanations

Children, and even many adolescents, are concrete thinkers: If they can't see something, feel it, taste it, smell it, or hear it, they have a hard time learning about it. Keep in mind that most sexual and reproductive organs and processes are invisible; they happen on or in bodies that aren't built like your own, or inside your own body where they can't be seen. (And many reproductive concepts—like the all-important female menstrual cycle—are total abstractions to a child.) Pictures and diagrams of the kind found in books written about the body for preschoolers and young children are indispensable.

Think Small

As your children grow up, don't worry excessively about how much they know about sexuality. More important will be how well they know what's most important to know, how easily they can talk about it, and whether they know how to acquire the additional information they may need in the future. With younger children, the same rules apply. Most important at this stage is that they come to see you as a ready source of answers to their immediate questions.

In answering a young child's questions, always try to start by giving a simple, direct, and of course accurate response. It's also a good idea to keep the response fairly general until you see how much detail he's interested in. For example: Your child notices a box of tampons for the first time and says, "What's that for?" You say, "That's something girls and women use when they get older." Then take a good look at the child's face. If he looks satisfied, you'll know you're probably done for the time being. If not, give a little more information or ask a general question about his response ("Did that answer your question?"). If more information is desired, you'll follow the "simple, direct, and accurate" rule again and again until the child is satisfied.

"Why do they need to use it?" suppose the child asks next.

"Because older girls and women have something called periods."

"What's a period?"

"It's something that happens once a month that tells a girl or woman she's not pregnant."

"Like what?"

"The uterus sends out some blood that it was storing up *just in case* there was a pregnancy, and now it's not needed. The tampon goes in the vagina and soaks it up."

Notice, by the way, how much easier conversations like these will go once the child has some baseline knowledge of body parts and functions!

Turn the Question back Before You Respond

Almost everyone has heard the very old joke about the child who asks, "Where did I come from," and causes the parents to jump into a frenzied rendition of sperm, eggs, penises, vaginas, and the like. At the end of the lengthy explanation, the child says, "That was really interesting, but Johnny says he comes from Chicago, and I just wanted to know where I was born."

Point well taken. When in doubt, or even as a general rule, ask a question back like "What do you mean?" before launching in. You might alternately start by asking the child the same question right back: "Where do you think you came from?" That often helps you get a handle right away on the real question or at least the wavelength the child is on.

Start with What the Child Already Knows

Once parent and child have a history of talking about sex and reproduction, as in the tampon story above, parents will appreciate how nicely each new concept fits with the last. Let's think back to the trilogy of questions we addressed in Chapter 3. Once the child knows the word *uterus* (where I come from), explaining about vaginas (how I got out of there) becomes quite simple if you remember to start by connecting the two logically and anatomically. "Do you remember a while ago when you asked where you came from and I told you about Mom's uterus? Well, right next to her uterus is another special place called her vagina and. . . . "

Looking for logical and historical connections in the child's conversational and learning history can make almost any subject explainable, at least on some basic level. As any teacher will tell you, it's one of the most challenging and fun things about watching and helping children learn.

Notice when you're tempted to leave stuff out

As many parents no doubt will acknowledge, sometimes they're tempted to take the "cheater's" way out when they get to a certain point in conversations with their children that they find uncomfortable. Not uncommonly, for example, when explaining reproduction to their children they might decide to leave out certain relevant but sensitive parts of the story altogether—like the little matter of the father's role or the fact that people have intercourse for reasons other than having babies.

There's certainly no need to rush into sharing these concepts, but when we happen to have a logical opening or the timing seems right, it's a good idea to mention rather than omit them. While saving us some momentary throat clearing, omissions may create misleading representations that can cause untold confusion for children later on, and the need for tricky backpedaling for us.

Remember that many times when we're tempted to say to a child, "You're not old enough to know that," what we really mean is that *we can't figure out how to explain it,* especially to someone so young. This line of thinking might also indicate simple rationalization on our part, enabling us to justify not talking about things that make us feel uncomfortable or anxious. In any case, it's a good idea to be honest with ourselves whenever we're tempted to be evasive and to try to work our feelings through. It will make us healthier sexual people ourselves, and better parents and teachers.

Notice when you're tempted to add stuff

Sometimes our need is the opposite—we feel compelled to add information and concepts to our explanations that the child is not really asking about. Since these extras are usually purely adult concepts, we often get hopelessly stuck trying to figure out how to explain them on the (nonexistent) child's level. When we get to the point where we're first explaining the concept of sexual intercourse, for example, we may suddenly feel it vitally necessary to throw in some high-sounding pronouncements about love, and marriage, and maturity, and feelings of intimacy, which for the child, at the moment, are not only too advanced but also totally irrelevant. The child, after all, is asking on the level of geography or transportation or causation and will not necessarily make the connections we are hoping for.

A young father I know shared an incident that taught him this lesson well. He had recently explained the concept of intercourse to his seven-year-old daughter, making it very clear that people *never, ever* do this unless and until they are married. The next night at the dinner table, his wife happened to mention that the couple next door was getting a divorce. When the little girl asked what the word *divorce* meant, her parents explained that they would no longer be married.

"Oh," was her only comment. "I guess that means Mr. Lane won't be putting his penis in Mrs. Lane's vagina anymore!"

By the way, I'm not implying at all that you can't introduce new concepts into a conversation, especially after you're sure you've heard the child out and given your full attention to her level of interest. You'd be wise, though, to check out your agenda in doing so (are you attempting to meet the child's needs or your own?) and to remind yourself that there's no great rush to tell the whole story at once. If we're doing a good job of simply tuning in to our child's current level of thought, especially early on, there will be plenty of time and opportunities later—when the child is ready for and naturally interested in more adult concepts—to elaborate.

There Are Some Subjects That Are Definitely Not Age Appropriate

Please do not interpret my emphasis on open and honest communication to mean that any and all subjects are appropriate to bring to the attention of young children. Sometimes, though, despite our best efforts, children are inadvertently exposed to topics that are beyond their years developmentally. More about how to handle these kinds of situations in Chapter 5.

How Do I Explain Sex Apart from Reproduction?

This is a question that I always encourage parents to think about very carefully. Unfortunately, it's one they often don't realize they need to think about at all.

Sadly, here's how most elementary and early adolescents will answer (usually after a lot of giggling) if you ask them to define the word *sex:* "Sex is when a man sticks his penis (or dick) in a woman's vagina (or hole)."

Just think for a minute about the language used to explain "the act" and what it communicates. Sex is something a man *does to* a woman—or, more accurately, something that *his* body part does to *her* body part. And that word *sticks* (which is almost always the verb of choice, even though their facial expression usually reflects their sense that it doesn't seem quite right)—does it in any way communicate that this is an experience of love, intimacy, caring, or mutuality—or any kind of humanity at all?

On another level, it's clear that in their minds the act of "sex" is equivalent to the act of "sexual intercourse," an equation that is both inaccurate and misleading. There are many ways that two people can relate to and enjoy each other's bodies sexually; one important example, but only one, is the act of sexual intercourse. Using language with children and adolescents in a manner that implies that sex equals intercourse, as we do constantly, is terribly confusing. Suppose we constantly used the word *Cheerios* whenever we were really referring to the food category *cereal,* the word *Miata* when we meant *car, burglary* when we meant *crime,* or *father* when we really meant *parent.* By confusing the example with the category, we'd be hampering children's ability to think clearly, rationally, and responsibly about the full range of possibilities. We'd also be conditioning them to think, by implication, that the one example we've constantly equated with its category is the best, the most important, and the only "real" example in the lot. In the case of the equation of sex with intercourse, we need only remind ourselves about the Clinton-Lewinsky scandal or the disturbing news that the majority of teenagers and even college students don't think of oral sex as *real* sex to understand the damaging fallout that results from this kind of linguistic nonsense.

You might be thinking, what does the Clinton-Lewinsky scandal or whatever a bunch of college kids happen to think about sex have to do with my five-year-old? This kind of distorted thinking starts that young (encouraged inadvertently by adults), and that's the point. And the earlier misconceptions are learned the harder they are to unlearn later.

The opposite—clear thinking about the meaning of *sex*, both linguistically and experientially—is easy to encourage in young children with simple common sense and a conscientious approach. When children as young as five or six ask questions about birth and conception, adults can be careful to use the phrase *sexual intercourse*, not the word *sex*, in explaining the processes involved in fertilization. (As we learned in Chapter 3, children's questions at this stage are not really about the meaning of sexual behavior anyway but about the mechanics of their origin.) Later on, parents can introduce the word *sex* whenever the time seems right to describe the more sophisticated and more adult concept of *sexual relating*. Sex, they can explain, is a very special, private, and pleasurable way that grownup couples—like moms and dads (or moms and moms, or dads and dads)—hold, kiss, and touch one another that makes them feel very close and loving. The specific details, and options, can be filled in gradually as the conversation continues to evolve.

Should I Bring up the Topic, Even If My Children Don't?

If there's something important you want your child to know about, and especially if you want to be the one to tell her or him about it first, you wouldn't hesitate to bring it up. If the subject is complex, like sex and reproduction, you'd probably have to give some thought to the best way to bring it up, but you wouldn't put it off. It's only because we tend to lose our good common sense about this particular subject (because we tend to imbue it with such irrational and potentially damaging power) that we become unnecessarily cautious. The old dictum "Best to wait until your child brings up the subject" should not become a hard-and-fast rule (truthfully, one of the main reasons to wait is that it makes things easier for nervous, inexperienced adults by giving them a helpful place to start). But remember, too, as we said before, there's no great emergency here either. If the child doesn't take the bait, or just plain isn't interested, there's no harm whatsoever in waiting.

What Can I Do to Encourage My Children to Ask Questions?

There are many natural and age-appropriate learning opportunities you can help create in your child's day-to-day life that will encourage spontaneous question asking. Remember, though, it's the openness you project and your obvious delight in your child's learning—about all of life's wonders, including this one—that is the biggest encouragement of all. Here are some concrete suggestions, many excerpted from Segal's *Your Child at Play: Three to Five Years.*

- Put a measuring tape on the wall and mark it for your child. Does she recognize that growing taller and getting older go together?
- Show your child her baby clothes. Talk about how small she was and how big she's grown.
- Show your child a family album. Can she find a picture of Mom and Dad when they were babies?
- Take your child to a farm and talk about baby animals.
- Read your child books about animals and their babies.
- When you are cooking dinner, talk about how chickens lay eggs or how milk comes from a cow. Show your child a seed inside a pumpkin and let him know that the seed will turn into a pumpkin.
- Give your child the opportunity to see and touch a newborn. Have her watch nursing and diaper changing. Visit the baby frequently and talk about its growth and development.

• Introduce your child to a pregnant woman and have him touch the woman's belly. Visit again and notice the woman and baby's growth. Visit once more after the delivery.

But, What If . . .

I've tried to include in the above discussion all of the most frequently asked parenting questions. Below are questions families commonly raise about some additional circumstances.

What If My Child Is Adopted or Was Conceived, Carried, or Delivered in an Alternative Way?

Regardless of the particular circumstances of their birth, almost all children were in fact conceived and born in the same way as almost all other children in the world. Parents of adopted children can feel free to answer questions about origins in the same matter-of-fact way we've been describing all along but taking care to speak in more general terms—for example, saying how babies grow in "the woman's uterus," not "their mother's uterus." (The second phrase could prove misleading, since it will be revealed at some point that babies can have more than one kind of mother.) The fact that these children now have adoptive parents as well as birth parents is an additional piece of information to be added to the story in whatever way, at whatever time, they've decided is right for their family.

Of course, many children in today's world were in fact *not* conceived or born in the traditional way, but the same principles apply. Children delivered by cesarean section, for example, can learn that most babies are born through their mother's vagina and that some are born through an opening that the doctor creates through the mother's abdominal wall. (Take care not to say "stomach"; that sets up incredibly confusing ideas and images for young children.)

In cases where children have been conceived in one of the various ways that require medical intervention, parents will need to make their own decisions about the depth of information they wish to provide and when they think it best to provide it. They can always begin, though, with the same basic steps we have described, with maybe a slight addition. When the child asks how babies are made, the parent can say, "Well, here's how it happens almost all the time." At the end of the explanation he or she can add, "Sometimes parents have trouble making babies this way, and a doctor has to help a sperm and egg come together. It's pretty complicated, but we can talk about that later sometime if you'd like." That strategy prepares the child for the concept of alternative methods of conception and opens the door to further conversation but doesn't necessarily require the parent to give details to the child about her or his particular conception (or gestation, in the case of surrogate parenting). That decision can then be made at a much later time.

Anne Bernstein's book *Flight of the Stork: What Children Think (and When) about Sex and Family Building* is a wonderful resource for families that were "built" in alternative ways.

What If My Child Goes Right Out and Tells Every Other Child At School or in the Neighborhood?

Fortunately, at about the same time that children are ready to learn the details of intercourse and reproduction, they are also old enough to firmly grasp the concept of privacy. They will be able to understand that this is very special and important information, so special in fact that other parents like to be the ones to tell their own children about it. "So," parents can say, "let's keep this information in our own family for now."

It's important to remember, too, that children are much less likely to willfully go around spreading information if they have learned it in a context that is positive, respectful, and open. When children learn from each other—amidst whispers and jokes that make them feel naughty and bold—they are much more likely to want to "show off" what they know.

We also have to stop and take a look, I think, at why we are so concerned about this issue in the first place. If we were to take it out of the context of sex, would we still mind children passing on interesting new information they have just learned about a pretty neat, in fact, downright fascinating and important, subject? Or is it perhaps *we* who think that there might be something "naughty" about children having this information at an early age? And if we don't think so, instead of trying to shield other children in the neighborhood or schoolyard from ours, shouldn't we be trying to help their parents understand that this is age-appropriate information for *all* children?

If we think realistically about the numbers of children who constantly pass on information about sex—more likely misinformation—in an atmosphere of silliness, disrespect, and even intimidation, why wouldn't we want the respectful, knowledgeable ones to get in on the act?

What If an Older Sibling Asks Questions within Earshot?

As for siblings overhearing conversations with older brothers and sisters, parents can simply relax; most of the time it's not a problem or issue at all. If the facts or ideas being discussed are beyond the younger child's understanding, they will merely whiz right by, and if not, the child will simply take away whatever information happens to seem interesting or appealing at the moment. The child might even ask a question or two at his or her level of comprehension, enjoying the opportunity to be included in such a serious and grownup conversation. Most importantly, what the child will also take away is the pleasant and comfortable hum of the background music that this kind of warm and open conversation creates in a family's life together. She or he will learn that this is a good and safe topic to bring up, no matter what or when.

On occasion, an older sibling might raise a topic or issue that is really scary or intense—for example, a news story about child sexual abuse or a sexual rumor about someone known to the family—which might make the parent nervous, and rightfully so, in the presence of a younger sibling. The older child in these circumstances needs the parent's undivided attention without the distraction of having to simultaneously translate or diffuse the issue on a level appropriate for the younger child. It's really good at these times if you and your older child have worked on a signal you can use to head off conversations that probably are best conducted out of earshot of younger sibs. In fact, these are situations your older child can be helped to feel really good about. "You're really growing up," you can say. "There will be times when we should talk by ourselves, just the two of us."

What If My Child Believes Misinformation or Concocts Inaccurate Theories?

In her wonderful book *The Emotional Life of the Toddler*, psychologist Alicia Lieberman tells the following story about Martin, a three-year-old, who asks his pregnant mother, "Mom, do you love the baby?" Martin's mother assures him she loves the baby very much. Martin now wants to know "Then why did you eat him?"

As Lieberman points out, a mother could be forgiven for giving her child a long explanation about how babies are made and born, but she compliments the mother for wisely choosing to answer only what Martin has asked. "I didn't eat him, Martin," she says. "My tummy is very big because babies grow inside their mommies' tummies." Martin says nothing more at this point, but two days later asks the next logical question, "Did I grow in your tummy, too?" Not until four months later, after his sister is born, does he think to ask, "How did she come out?"

Children ask questions piecemeal because they take their time making sense of each new piece of information they receive, as Lieberman reminds us. They know how much they can manage and will stop asking before they reach overload. Parents do well to respect this signal and not try to "undo" too quickly what might makes sense to the child at a given moment, even if it's inaccurate or outlandish factually. If we keep the channels of communication open and if they sense our patience, they'll keep coming back for more information and further refinement.

As my mother used to say whenever I was particularly exasperated by my children's "immature" thinking or behavior, "What's the chance, do you think, that they'll still be doing that or thinking that when they're twenty-one?"

What If My Child Has a Negative Reaction to Information He's Been Told?

Most often, as children receive each new piece of information about their origins, their spoken or unspoken reaction is pretty much like Martin's: "Oh." Much to their parents' amazement (because, of course, we're the ones who make such a big deal about all of this), they simply take it all in stride. To them, learning new things, no matter the topic, is all in a day's work.

All children are different, of course, and parents can expect a big range of "normal" reactions. Some children are decidedly bland and blasé and will look at you with blank, uninterested faces (while you're sitting there sweating bullets). Others will be fascinated and will want you to repeat what you've told them over and over just for the fun of hearing it again. Some will listen in rapt attention for a while, then quickly lose interest, and may even change the subject

midsentence. Many children will react physically rather than verbally and begin to engage in exaggerated play behavior that imitates
what they've been told. A few children will find the whole thing
hysterically funny, and others will simply refuse to believe it or think
their parents are putting them on with ridiculous made-up stories.
And some will react with shock or disgust—"Oh, sick, gross!"

No matter what our child's reaction, we'll do best if we learn to
take a page out of their own book and simply try to take it all in
stride. (If you're feeling particularly reactive because the child's
response is a negative one, try to remember my mother's great
advice in the last section!) Regardless of the child's individual reaction, it's always a good idea to reflect for her what you're observing: "I see you're having trouble believing all this"; "You find this
stuff really interesting!"; "You're getting pretty bored, I think"; "You
find this whole thing pretty disgusting, huh?" That's a great way to
normalize their reaction—and the topic itself—and let your child
know that, as always, you're vitally interested in him or her and his
or her feelings.

What If I Get Really Stuck?

As we've seen, parents can find it enormously liberating when
they come to understand that a young child's questions about sex
and reproduction are really just "same ol', same ol'" questions about
geography, transportation, and causation. Whenever parents are
really stuck about what to say or do about any other sexuality-
related topic, my advice is the same: Find a way to reframe the
issue in a nonsexual context.

An example from my own life: When my older son was about
four, he asked if he could play with some of the tampons in the
bathroom. He wanted to put them in the sink, watch them fill up
with water, and pull them around like boats. I had a ridiculously
hard time with this request and obsessed over it for days; I just

didn't know if this was a "proper" game for a four-year-old boy. Finally, I remember asking myself: If there were another object in the house that was this harmless, this inexpensive, this disposable, this much fun to play with—and could at the same time teach a lesson about Archimedes's Principle—would I even hesitate? I went out and bought him his own box.

What If I've Already Blown It?

There are almost always parents who come up at the end of my workshops to ask nervously about a particular thing they've said or done, or not said or done, just to make sure they haven't "blown it" entirely and ruined their child forever. Relax, I try to tell them, you've done just fine, and even if you didn't, there's always tomorrow. The thing about parenting is that your children are always still there in the morning for an instant "do over." You can *always* go back and say, "you know, I really don't like the way I handled this or that. Can I try it again?" They'll love and appreciate you even more for your honesty and willingness to make yourself so vulnerable. And you'll help take the pressure off of everyone to have to be so perfect all the time.

Taking Time to Refresh Your Memory

At the end of this book, you'll find a section that contains basic information about anatomy and physiology of the sexual and reproductive systems and some general health facts that all adults should know (and, sadly, many if not most don't). Even if you're sure you're pretty well informed, I can almost guarantee you'll learn something new. Most importantly, it will give you some ideas about how to present information clearly and accurately to your children in ways that will help them build their knowledge base in a helpful, logical pace and order.

5

Oh, No! What Do
I Do Now?

Years ago, a friend told me a story about her four-year-old and about expecting the unexpected.

She and her son were shopping in a local department store. She looked down for only a second to check a price, and when she turned around he was nowhere to be seen. Frantic, she dashed around the clothing racks, yelling his name, "Eric! Eric! I'm very frightened. Where are you?"

A couple of sections over, thank goodness, he finally answered her calls: "I'm busy, Mom."

Still, she couldn't see him. "Eric Matthew Fisher! Don't tell me you're busy. Where are you!"

"I'm busy, Mom. I want to feel her nipples!"

She turned and followed his voice to the next department over—lingerie. Eric had climbed up on a pedestal, where he could just about reach the mannequin's shoulder. He had removed her spaghetti string strap and was blithely standing there, swiping her right nipple intently with his palm.

"Oh, my God! What did you say?," I asked.

"GET DOWN!"

"Good move," I said.

"That's just what my husband said—right after he asked which branch store it was, the one across town or the one around the corner."

Curiosity: A Child's Ticket to the World

In Chapter 4, we examined the steady intellectual development that spurs a child's insistent curiosity about the wonders of her or his universe, including the process of creation.

The keenness of a young child's curiosity, of course, is only partly intellect; it expresses itself not only in the workings of the mind but alternatively through the senses, emotions, relationships, movements, and behavior. There is so much to learn, so much to explore—physically, emotionally, socially, and intellectually. No wonder young children are in such perpetual motion! No wonder, like Eric, they're so "busy."

For children, curiosity about sexuality is understandably intense because sexuality itself is intense: It involves the mind, the senses, the emotions, relationships, movements, *and* behavior. (Add procreation, gender roles, identity, body image, health concerns, morality, religion, law, politics, and aging, and it's no surprise that sexuality continues to remain intense for most people throughout their lives.) Parents can expect that children's sexual curiosity will take many forms and find expression in almost every aspect of family life. In this chapter we'll address some of the most common, and the most challenging.

Gender Differences: "Boys Are Fancy on the Outside, Girls Are Fancy on the Inside"

With characteristic simplicity and respectfulness, the beloved Mr. Rogers got it just right with this low-key, reassuring way of telling boys and girls how they're made and how, even though they're different, they're each uniquely special.

As early as fifteen months old, it's not unusual for toddlers to become very interested in noticing body differences and sometimes even to show visible upset or concern over what body parts they do or do not have. By eighteen months, most begin to show signs that they recognize themselves in the mirror; at about the same time, they begin to use the pronouns *I, me,* and *mine* and even proper names to refer to themselves. As Alicia Lieberman points out, these observations suggest that toddlers are now able to experience themselves objectively, as people who can be seen from the outside, as well as felt from the inside. As a direct result, they become both more self-aware and more interested in their appearance, and this new fascination leads naturally to a heightened curiosity about sexual organs—their own and others'. Once again, their seeming interest in SEX! is simply a part of the larger developmental whole.

When there are other small children who are easily accessible (sibs, cousins, friends, etc.) who can be diaper changed and can bathe, dress, and go to the bathroom together, the whole process of explaining male/female differences usually goes rather smoothly. Comparisons with moms' and dads' bodies are also helpful and inevitable, though they can may make for a little more discomfort on the adult's part or add a few complicating variables: "But how come yours is so big!?" "How come you have hair and I don't?"

Often children don't just want to talk and ask, they want to touch and look—very close up; it's helpful to remember that that's how they learn best and not to take it personally. Some parents won't mind such close scrutiny, and others can simply and calmly decline while acknowledging the child's curiosity and their own sense of privacy in a positive way. (They can always then take a trip to the library to get children's picture books on the subject instead.) Children at this stage are also very uninhibited about noticing such things in public—at exotic locations like zoos ("Look at the penis on that elephant, will you!") and mundane ones like supermarkets ("Does that woman have a vagina like you do mom?"). A gentle but firm reminder about being sensitive to other people's feelings would be appropriate in either instance (with the explanation in the first case that, though the animals won't mind at all, the people standing nearby might!).

Parents should also not be alarmed if confusion or downright upset persists in their children about what they and others have or don't have "down there." Many young children maintain a stubborn skepticism about what they've been told about such differences; they may continue to insist that girls and women really do or did have a penis, which they are either concealing or have somehow "lost" presumably because of some accident or even punishment. (Boys are more apt to be anxious about this issue, for obvious reasons; girls may also be continually, but more purely, curious.) Both boys and girls will often play at being the other gender: Boys will try to tuck their penises away; girls may want to tape some sort of object to their vulva. Part of this behavior is playacting, and part longing or wishful thinking, but most of it is probably a simple indication of their relatively immature level of cognitive sophistication about *gender constancy*.

Though boys and girls begin to have a clear sense of their gender as early as eighteen months, in their minds male/female dynamics and dichotomies are not viewed in nearly the same way as adults understand them. Many children think of gender as being quite fluid; they truly believe that they can be both mommies and daddies when they grow up, or can have a mixture of male and female organs if they want, and/or can grow up to marry both or either of their parents if that's what suits them. As Alicia Lieberman says, at this stage, "everybody wants to have everything!" Toddlers and preschoolers may certainly have a good sense of *gender roles*—the social expectations of what girls and boys are supposed to be like and do—but their permanent and internalized sense of *gender identity* (what gender I am, now and forever) will not solidify until later on. Parents will do well at this earlier point to understand this unique worldview, avoid criticism of their children's fluid interpretations in all of its various forms and manifestations, and be patient yet firm in gently pointing out the realities of the true situation.

About Language:
Poop, Doody, Weewee, and No. 1?

Actually, Mr. Rogers got it *almost* right. Girls are fancy on the inside *and* on the outside, and boys are fancy on the *inside*, too.

In the early 1980s, I participated in a workshop attended by about seventy-five sexuality educators. One of the topics we discussed was sexual language. In small groups we were asked to identify all of the words we had ever heard for various sexual organs and processes. The word that generated the longest collective list by far (we gave up at a hundred) was the word *penis;* the shortest, *clitoris.* Not long after, I watched a segment of a *Donahue* talk show on which two sex therapists were discussing female sexual anatomy and mentioned the importance of the nerve-packed and highly arousable clitoris (the first time the word had been mentioned on TV, to my knowledge). I learned later that the switchboard apparently was lit up for hours after the show ended by adult viewers calling in to ask, "What's a clitoris?"

Female bodies are indeed very fancy on the outside, and the outside sexual organs even have a special name, *vulva. Vulva* is a collective term for all of the external female genitalia (as *face* is a collective term for the eyes, nose, and mouth). It includes the inner and outer labia, or lips, surrounding the vaginal and urethral openings; the clitoris (an organ that can be described as "bump"-like, located at the top of the inner labia); and the mons (the mound of skin on top of the pubic bone where pubic hair eventually grows).

Many girls and women, in truth, have never even heard the word *vulva* and can barely name any of the organs which compose it. This ignorance of female body parts and the names that describe them harkens to the days when women's organs were considered "dirty" and shameful. And, since the function of these little-known organs is primarily sexual, not reproductive, ignorance of them also reflects a time in our history when "good" and "normal" girls and women were considered incapable of sexual feelings—*ever.*

There's an even more fundamental confusion in the minds of most girls and boys, and probably many adult men and women: The vagina, contrary to popular opinion, is *NOT* located on the *outside* of the female anatomy. The vagina is an *internal* pouch—really just a potential space—located just inside the vaginal opening. Thinking that the vagina is located somewhere on the outside or that it is both inside *and* outside, as many people do, is tantamount to not knowing the difference between your face and your throat!

For the more than thirty years I've been teaching, it's been clear that neither males nor females know much at all about the internal male parts. I think this lack of information derives from a time when most "sex education" was really "period education"; as a result, many adults have never really been required to learn formally about the male reproductive system. Even today, the children and adolescents that I teach—both girls and boys—are often incredibly confused about such basic concepts as the difference between sperm and semen, or erections and ejaculations. And terms such as *vas deferens, seminal vesicle,* and *prostate gland* (an organ which is mentioned frequently in the news today) are not even in their memory banks. Clearly, we need to be doing a better job of educating *everybody* about *everything.*

In case you're getting worried, I'm not at all suggesting that parents even attempt to teach all of these terms to their young children, only that they keep these common gaps and misconceptions in mind as their children grow and learn. But, I would strongly suggest that, in explaining male/female differences, parents start by relaying that boys have a penis and girls have a vulva (as opposed to a vagina). Some parents may also want to teach their daughters (and sons) the word *clitoris,* and that is certainly appropriate. Little boys certainly know the name for the organ that is capable of giving them pleasurable sexual sensations; little girls certainly can know the name for the comparable part of their body, too.

We'll need to prepare ourselves to give accurate and straightforward information as we gradually help toddlers and preschoolers learn the names for a growing number of body parts and functions. To become a normal part of their everyday vocabulary, words like *penis, testicles, scrotum, erection, vulva, labia, clitoris, vagina, urethra, urinate, anus,* and *bowel movement* will need to become an everyday part of ours. And in case you're thinking that those big words are simply too long and complicated for small children to master, I am reminded of the time when one of my boys came home from preschool excited to explain how he had *laminated* all of his pictures in art class that day. Any three-year-old who can so effortlessly learn to say "laminate" can certainly handle the word *urinate.*

For many of us this kind of openness and directness will necessitate homework and practice. Many parents find it convenient and probably less embarrassing to slide into the use of babyish expressions or pet family names for body parts and functions—like the common ones in the heading for this section on language. For several reasons, I always encourage the use of "proper" terms instead. First, I think we should avoid teaching children information or language that they will have to unlearn and replace later on. Second, I think using dictionary terms teaches an underlying respect for the body and its functions—and the message that sexual parts in most ways are just like all other body parts—whereas babyish or other forms of slang can encourage the idea that the sexual parts (and their neighbors) are fundamentally different at best, even bad or disgusting at worst. They also may promote silliness and an unnecessary fascination with scatological humor. (Children will be exposed to plenty of this later on from peers; getting a different foundation at home will help diffuse its power and impact.) Finally, slang of any kind is what I would call "indirect" language; slang words "stand for" other words and in a sense are a form of code. Using "real" terms instead reinforces the idea that direct, up-front communication about sexuality is the best policy.

If you do decide to take the direct route, you may also need to do some explaining to your children's grandparents, aunts, uncles, baby-sitters, and day care providers, and these conversations may well require a good deal of courage. Remarkably, even in the twenty-first-century United States, many of these words are considered taboo—if not explicitly counterculture—terms. As a woman in one of my parenting groups said recently, "Oh my God, I couldn't *possibly* teach those words to my daughter. What if she were to repeat them in front of my mother, or worse yet, what if she were to say them at school! I can't be expected to change culture all by myself!"

Well, yes and no. For our children, especially when they are still very young, *we and our immediate family are their culture*. Language is a potent conveyor of attitudes and values, not just information. Parents will need to decide what attitudes and values they want to instill and recognize that their choice of language can either rein-force or contradict those messages in powerful ways. Parents will also need to reflect honestly on whose needs they are really attempting to meet—their own need to avoid embarrassment or recrimination or their child's need to acquire an accurate, direct, and respectful language for thinking and communicating about the sexual parts of their anatomy and eventually the sexual parts of their lives.

Teaching about body parts, functions, and differences using direct and precise language also sets the stage handily for respond-ing much more easily to the sequence of questions young children will typically begin to ask about their origins. I remember how well this approach worked with my second son when he was four. One day, having noticed a box of tampons in my bathroom, he asked what they were for. When I explained that older girls and women used them when they were grown up, he asked why boys couldn't use them, too. It turned out to be a great opening for talking about openings—which ones boys and girls have and don't have and where they are located. Some time later, as a result, answering his questions about origins followed much more easily and logically. In fact, with the help of additional information and some diagrams, he gradually pretty much figured out the whole thing all by himself!

Genital Touching: "But It Feels Soooo Good!"

Even infants, once they have developed the requisite motor ability, delight in finding and touching their genitals, just as they do their eyes, nose, mouth, ears, and navel. During the toddler years, especially as diapers are discarded and the sexual parts become more dependably accessible (Wow! a new toy!), genital touching often continues spontaneously and sporadically as an interesting and fun pastime (as anyone who's ever watched an ecstatic three-year-old boy yanking on his penis like it's a piece of taffy—and been tempted to intervene before he pulls the thing off entirely—can attest). Later, by the age of four or five, the behavior often takes on a more purposeful quality. Rubbing on the genitals or rubbing them against a handy object may become something the child chooses to do more frequently and more consciously because it feels pleasurable, relaxing, and soothing.

All of these behaviors are normal, expected, and entirely harmless. I repeat: All of these behaviors are normal, expected, and entirely harmless. Pardon me for reiterating, but I'm in the habit of saying this statement at least twice because, even though people "know" this fact today, deep down inside I'm not sure they truly believe it. My middle- and high-school students, for example, ask all the time: "I know masturbation is okay, but is it *really* okay?" They are also absolutely incredulous—and tremendously grossed out—to hear that babies and young children would actually touch themselves in this way. But perhaps their reactions should not surprise us. What kind of attitude might we expect to persist even today about a behavior that's been attached to a linguistic handle (dating back thousands of years) that means, literally, "to defile oneself?"

Although most parents speak about masturbation tolerantly today and are relatively laissez faire in their approach, it remains a complicated, embarrassing, and anxiety-producing topic for many. It's one they tend to avoid talking about with their children unless an incident occurs which prompts or requires it.

Once again, I think it is our collective ignorance about sexuality as a culture that is partially the source of these negative and uncomfortable feelings. The body's sexual system—unlike the reproductive system, which acquires mature form and function only after puberty—is fully present and functional at birth, a biological fact of life that surprises almost all adults. Babies' bodies, therefore, are quite capable of sexual feelings even to the point of orgasm. (Some parents in fact have observed their young children moving and breathing rhythmically in the throes of an obvious sexual climax.) Baby boys experience frequent erections, and in baby girls sexual lubrication regularly passes through the walls of the vagina. Indeed, both of these reactions occur involuntarily every ninety minutes during sleep throughout our entire lives.

Many children are quite casual about touching and rubbing their genitals and will do so in front of others without inhibition or even awareness. Infants and toddlers, too young to understand social convention, are just following their impulses. In the case of older children, they are simply spending time "being with" themselves in their own little world, often oblivious to the fact that other people may be around. Especially if they are overtired or bored—or they're feeling sad, scared, sick, lonely, or left out—they'll often stroke their genitals for comfort or to distract themselves. Sometimes it may be a sign that they've had an unusually exciting or tense day or, if the frequency seems on the increase, an indication that they're experiencing a stressful developmental period.

In many instances the motivation is pure and simple pleasure. During ordinary physical activities, children happen upon experiences all the time—rubbing on poles, sliding on banisters, straddling animals, hobbyhorses, or amusement park rides—that stimulate pleasurable genital sensations. Their delight as they choose to repeat these activities again and again is obvious to anyone paying attention. Even the need to urinate can provide sexual stimulation. One little boy, obviously needing to "go," was standing in the family room holding onto his erect penis for dear life. When asked if he wanted to use the potty, he thought about it for a minute and declined. "No thanks," he said, "It feels too good!"

Once children are old enough to grasp the concept of privacy, parents can begin to help them understand that touching or enjoying their genitals is healthy and normal but something people do in private. Usually a few gentle reminders will suffice. Before that stage, parents will need to deal with their children's lack of inhibition in ways that feel comfortable for them or others who may be aware of the behavior but that demonstrate respect for the child's need to feel good about his or her body and the sensations it can produce. Some will choose to ignore what's happening, not caring about it one way or the other or knowing that the child will soon become distracted by some other fun or interesting thing to do. Others will feel comfortable commenting directly to the child: "That feels good, doesn't it?" Others might want to calmly pick her up and distract her with some other activity. Most important is to avoid communicating to the child any sense of shame or condemnation for enjoying this harmless form of self-discovery.

In some families, there is another aspect of this issue that will need to be addressed. Religion is an important source of guidance about sexuality for many parents, and in some cases their religion may teach that masturbation in any form is extremely negative and even sinful. I would encourage them to take into account that genital touching in young children has a very different meaning and context than masturbation in adolescence or adulthood. It will be very difficult to stop the behavior at this young age without instilling negative feelings about the body and about sexuality in general. Developmentally, parents would do best to wait to discourage it, if they feel they must, until the child is old enough to understand the religious doctrine behind the prohibition and why the parents consider it so important.

Sex Play: "Show Me Yours, I'll Show You Mine!"

Cultural attitudes about various forms of sexual play among young children have also become more open and accepting in recent decades. Said one young father recently, "I don't care about it at all, as long as my daughter gets an equal shot at playing the doctor *and* the nurse!"

Nonetheless, parents who stumble onto children examining one another in various states of undress are sometimes quite unnerved by the experience. As in the case of genital touching, they may *know* it's okay but may not have accepted on a deeper emotional level that it's *really* okay. Moreover, in a society where child sexual abuse has become so publicized and where children are exposed to so many adult-oriented images and conversations about sex, some parents are ever on guard for signs of unhealthy sexual influences and behaviors.

As always in sorting out these kinds of mixed feelings and concerns, it's useful to have a clear sense of the normal and expected parameters of child behavior.

Young children, ever curious about their own bodies (exhibit A), view other peoples' bodies as exhibits B, C, and D. They are fascinated by similarities and differences because comparison is their modus operandi for understanding and classifying the world around them. They may become especially interested in parts of the body that are usually kept covered, since there are so many fewer opportunities for satisfying that particular curiosity. How very clever of them to "invent" spontaneous games like "doctor" to get unsuspecting specimens (e.g., friends, peers, siblings, cousins) to disrobe in such a socially acceptable manner!

Should parents happen upon such a game in progress, they have a number of healthy options. Some will simply choose to walk away unnoticed or, if they have been spotted, say, "Excuse me," and turn and leave, trusting in the children's healthy instincts and curiosity. (The fact that children tend to play these games privately and in the context of games that have clearly defined roles and rules is a telling indication that they already have already internalized a healthy sense of limits about these kinds of activities; the less parents interfere—and attach unnecessary hype and attention—the more quickly the curiosity will pass.) Other parents, especially if they are unsure of the other families' views on the subject, may want to say something like "We keep our clothes on when we have company" and then encourage the children to get dressed and move on to other kinds of activities where their play can be more easily observed. No matter what option they select, parents can always choose to use the incident as a teachable moment. Later, while acknowledging the children's curiosity in an accepting and positive tone, they can offer to answer questions and give information: "I can see that you are interested in how people's bodies are made. That's a really neat subject! Let's talk about it."

Many parents, even those who know to expect sexual play as a basically normal and healthy activity, are still quite shocked and stymied when it's *their child* who's involved, especially if she or he appears to be the "instigator." (Truthfully, somebody always has to come up with the idea first, and as long as there is no unhealthy coercion going on and everyone involved is participating happily, there are no real "instigators"; it's pretty fruitless to think or talk in those terms, especially when informing or discussing the situation with other children's parents.) Don't worry if you're ever taken totally off guard: If you've worked through your attitudes and any residual negativity or anxiety left over from your own upbringing about this behavior, you're still likely to do well even if you don't handle the situation in the exact way you might have hoped for or imagined. One mother I know entered the children's bedroom when her family and another were away at the beach together and confronted her five-year-old straddling the other family's child while rubbing on his penis. She froze in place, not able to think of a thing to say. Finally, she blurted out the only idea that came to mind: "David, I told you NOT to play on the bed!" It worked like a charm.

In Chapter 7, you'll find guidelines that are helpful in detecting the tiny minority of situations and contexts in which sexual activity among young children might truly be unhealthy or even indicate a history of abuse. Most important to keep in mind are the qualities that characterize healthy, normal childhood exploration. Here are some of the most important ones, several delineated by Toni Cavanaugh Johnson in her very helpful book *Understanding Your Child's Sexual Behavior: What's Natural and Healthy*.

- Children involved in healthy, natural sexual play are generally of similar age, size, and developmental level, and these behaviors typically occur between children who have an ongoing mutual play relationship. Siblings less frequently engage one another in this kind of exploration, probably because they instinctively know Mom or Dad might disapprove; the "secret" could be tattled at any time as a way of getting the other child "in trouble."

- Though many children engage in sexual play, especially between the ages of four and six, many do not. Both groups of children are inherently healthy. Statistically, as many girls as boys are involved, and childhood sexual exploration occurs as frequently between same-gender children as between boys and girls. Who is chosen is typically a practical matter of who your friends happen to be, who is willing, and who is available at the time the idea strikes.

- Children engaged in normal sexual play do so lightheartedly and with a spirit of fun, adventure, and even giddy excitement. When asked by an adult to stop and redirect their play to another activity, they agree with little fuss. The behavior may stop altogether—or at least until the children reach a new plateau of interest some time in the future—or the children just might work harder next time to keep their activities hidden from adults. Parents who are uncomfortable with the behavior continuing might want to provide additional supervision and structure during playtime.

- Healthy childhood play occurs in the absence of pressure; even the timeworn expression "I'll show you mine if you show me yours" is indicative of the sense of mutuality and fair play inherent in normal sexual play. Sometimes the invitation might *sound* coercive—"I'll be your best friend if you show me yours"—but such expressions are typical of how little children operate in healthy peer relationships and must be interpreted within the framework of a child's unique developmental level.

- Even though children's sexual behaviors might look like adult sexual behaviors, they are not experienced in the same way. What drives the activity is not a desire for intimacy and sexual gratification but an interest in exploring body characteristics, similarities, and differences. (Even though some children might feel sexual pleasure or arousal, it's a sideshow to the main attraction; also, their excitement may have as much to do with doing something perceived as forbidden as with its sexual aspects.) Moreover, the choice of the same or other gender as a playmate in these circumstances bears no relationship to later sexual orientation. (Once again, this activity is fundamentally about *curiosity* drive, not *sex* drive.)

Sex Talk: What about *#$#@*#?

The issue of "appropriate" sexual language is a confusing and challenging one for children. As they grow up, they'll be required to learn not one but several different languages for body parts and processes related to sex and elimination: *babyish language, slang, dictionary,* and *common* or *"polite" discourse.* Even more demanding, they'll need eventually to master the intricacies and subtleties of a slew of unwritten double, triple, and even quadruple standards currently in place for determining exactly who is allowed to use what kinds of words where, when, and under what circumstances.

As an example: They'll need to decipher a complex (and regionally variable) set of codes dictating that while babies *peepee* in their diapers, and boys at school *take a whiz* in the *john* with their *dicks,* girls *make sissy* with their *weewee* in the *little girls' room;* that doctors will want them to *urinate* in cups, will check their *penis* or *vagina,* poke around in their *groin,* and maybe put a thermometer or suppository in their *rectum* (but that Uncle Bill is an *asshole*); and that moms, when at home, will use the *bathroom* to *pee* (and only occasionally to take a bath) but, at nice restaurants, will get up to use the *powder room* to—well, what exactly do moms do in a powder room, anyway?

Ridiculous, isn't it?

We don't simply confuse children with this linguistic mess (How come Mom and Dad say "shit!" when they're mad but "BM" when they're really making one? What do "Fuck you!" and "screwing" have to do with "making love"? What is "69" and is there a number "70"? Why are whole people called "dickheads"?). We also communicate (and pass on) our culture's fundamental ambivalence and anxiety about sexual parts and functions and their close cousins, the organs and functions connected with excretion and elimination. And whenever adults communicate ambivalence—especially when we also communicate a reluctance to communicate about it—we invite ambivalence, testing, and values confusion in children and adolescents.

Adults can take the power, confusion, and ambivalence out of sexual language by being direct in their own personal usage. We can also refrain from referring to sexual language as "dirty" language (a phrase that communicates that sex itself is dirty) and let children know that there are no intrinsically "bad" or "good" words: Virtually all words can be used in bad ways that can really hurt people's feelings or in good ways that can make them feel good. Although adults should encourage the use of proper terminology about sexual and related terms (my recommended policy, as you know), we shouldn't hesitate to talk about slang terms with children if they arise in conversation or are overheard. Explaining slang terms and why many people find them offensive is a great way of talking about the values that are important to us as individuals and as parents. It will also help children demystify the "codes" referred to above and understand why we have them.

And ultimately, we'll reduce children's fascination—sometimes to the point of preoccupation—with sexual terminology and lessen their need and ability to use sexual terms to shock or hurt others, since the language will no longer be as taboo and thereby enticing.

Toilet Training: "All This Fuss, and Now You Want Me to Flush It?"

A complete discussion of the topic of toilet training is beyond the purview of this book. Given the close proximity of the sexual and elimination systems, however, and the similar ways in which our culture assigns language and attitudes to these body parts and processes, a few comments are in order.

Starting in the second year of life, toddlers become increasingly aware of the sphincters that control urination and bowel movements. Eventually, with the help of looking and touching, they are better able to differentiate all of the various body parts and openings in the groin and the sensations (and products) they can produce. (Parents may notice a good bit of *internal* exploring at this stage as well, many children attempting to put fingers or other objects into their various orifices, with great delight and interest.) All of these new levels of learning and awareness help set the stage for them eventually—and in their own time—to participate cooperatively in the process of toilet training.

Toileting, of course, presents challenges for both parents and their toddlers. Parents must learn to gauge their child's readiness and provide encouragement and support but not undue pressure. Toddlers must learn to master all the necessary steps—recognizing their body sensations, calling a parent or caretaker, managing the toilet or potty seat, timing the release of their urine and feces correctly—and conquer more than a few formidable fears: Oh, no! Will I make it? Will Daddy be mad? Will I fall in? What if I have to do both? Will I ever get flushed away like my BMs? Along the way, everyone will experience a variety of mishaps and frustrations, at least a few battles, and eventually, the excitement, relief, and sense of pride and accomplishment that will come with success. (Those of you who at the moment are in severe doubt about that last assertion, remember my mother's advice: Is wearing diapers something they'll probably still be doing when they're twenty-one?)

Parents will need to be patient and also recognize their children's conflicts with issues of dependence versus independence, of "holding on" versus "letting go"—making toileting a perfect metaphor actually for the entire toddler stage. We can help by remaining, or at least seeming, as calm, detached, and positive as possible about both the processes and the products involved. Children see urine and feces as fascinating, even cherished extensions of themselves; parents who comment with excessive disgust about odors, consistencies, grossness, or other admittedly unpleasant features send unnecessarily negative and possibly confusing messages. Especially for girls, whose sexual parts are in such close proximity to their urethral and anal openings, overly negative attitudes about germs and odors can easily become generalized to the entire area and create extreme self-consciousness—to the point of disgust and even self-loathing—that can take an obvious toll on sexual self-concept and later sexual functioning.

A final plea to all parents: Please help children understand—both boys and girls—that female bodies have *three* openings in the area between their legs *(urinary, vaginal,* and *anal).* They also should know that these openings are connected to three different systems *(urinary, reproductive,* and *digestive)* that are not joined in any way either structurally or functionally. (These points can be made gradually and over time, but children should certainly know this information by the early primary grades.) I cannot begin to tell you the number of children, teens, and adults I teach who have no clue about how their bodies are made "down there" and how the various parts and systems fit (or don't fit) together; in fact, most think that their reproductive, digestive, and urinary systems are somehow blended together. (Actually, in males, the urinary and reproductive systems do overlap but only partially.) It's very difficult to help them unlearn these misperceptions and relearn the correct information later on. Take my word for it: Sexuality, health, and biology teachers across the United States will bless you!

Nudity/Privacy:
"No, You *Cannot* Watch!"

In all my years of professional experience, I don't think I've come across any topic where family rules and experiences vary more than they do around the issue of nudity. I have a great deal of respect for this diversity of views and almost always encourage parents to heed their own instincts about their privacy concerns.

Nudity, by definition, is intensely personal. It reveals parts of us that we show only a relative handful of people our whole lives. Each of us comes to adulthood—and parenthood—with varying degrees of comfort with our bodies and with "letting it all hang out," so to speak. Our earliest and therefore most immutable teachings play a powerful role in the rules and meanings we come to associate with nudity and privacy, as do our most deeply felt assessments of how well our bodies "measure up" to the standards, often quite harsh, we've learned to self-impose.

Babies, of course, know of no such boundaries and evaluations. In fact, part of the ongoing socialization process is teaching young children appropriate rules about privacy and modesty. The closeness and intimacy of family life provide literally countless opportunities for teaching and learning about the processes of covering and uncovering as children experience the thousands and thousands of daily activities that are centered around bathing, changing, dressing, nursing, toileting, and sleeping.

The particular rules about when and when not to cover up vary dramatically from family to family and seem to depend most heavily on the ages and genders of the children and on the unique constellation of personal attitudes and feelings individual parents bring to the new family unit. Eventually, as children grow older and their own natural sense of personal modesty begins to evolve—probably as a reflection of advancing developmental needs for separateness and independence—their feelings and attitudes, as well, become important factors in the mix.

The one rule I encourage all parents to adopt is to follow their basic "gut" sense in drawing privacy lines. Though it is probably very healthy for young children (especially before age four) to experience "nakedness" as a normal and natural state of being and there need be no special limits, some parents will find that they are unable to feel relaxed in the nude around their children at any age. So long as the attitude communicated is a need for privacy—and not a sense of shame or disgust—there is no harm done in remaining covered at all times. In fact, I think that forcing yourself to be "liberated" when it doesn't suit your style, in an attempt to encourage a child's "comfort," is likely to backfire anyway. Of course, if a parent is decidedly uncomfortable with his or her own discomfort and knows there might be important issues to work through about body image or nudity that are impacting life in other ways, getting professional help or guidance would probably be wise.

What seems to work well for most families is relying on the parents' sense of when individual children are too big or too old to go au naturel. Everybody delights in watching the utter adorableness of a very small child running around blissfully naked. Once she turns four or five, however, this kind of attention begins to feel like an infringement on the child's personhood now that she is no longer "just" a little baby and is coming into her own individual and more autonomous self. Some children even at this age spontaneously begin to show signs of modesty (wanting to dress and toilet in private) and to communicate signals that they're less comfortable around Mom and/or Dad's nudity. (Other parents and children are still comfortable being nude around each other well into the child's elementary school years.) Knowing when to draw the curtain is most often something you just sense—a certain look, a sense of tension, a joke, a comment, a diverting of the eyes—that tells you it's time to set a limit: "Big girls wear clothes when other people are around" or "Now that you're getting so big and don't need mom or dad to watch you all the time, please make sure you knock on the (bathroom or bedroom) door if you need something."

Parents can use the same kinds of low-key messages and calm tone when they sense that siblings are getting too big to comfortably bathe together. And they can use the same kind of "comfort thermometer" to decide when touching a child—or being touched by one—on or near a sexual part of the body begins to feel uncomfortable for either.

Parents wonder, too, about what to do if a child happens to come upon them while they are engaged in sexual activity. There is no harm in children understanding that parents share a special way of being physically intimate with one another (in fact, it's probably very healthy). True, such an experience is likely to be disconcerting or embarrassing, for both parents and children, but the best approach again is to try to remain calm and matter-of-fact. Parents can say that they are having some private time together and would like the child to leave the room and be sure to close the door (and to please knock when it is closed in the future). Then, it's probably best for one of the adults to go to the child to ask what she saw— or thought she saw (younger children, especially, may interpret the behavior as angry or aggressive)—and to invite questions or offer reassurance about what has happened.

Age *In*appropriateness: *What* Did You Say?

A kindergarten teacher stopped me in the hall one day to tell me a funny—or not-so-funny (she wasn't sure which)—story about a five-year-old in her class. It was several months into the Clinton-Lewinsky debacle, and she had overheard the girl talking to another child about the "president's candle." "What the heck?" the teacher said to herself, making a rather adult sexual association to the word *candle*. Worrying about what the children had been exposed to, she listened in more intently. It soon became clear (as she had a good laugh at herself) that the girls were talking about the president's *'candal*, as in "scandal," not his "candle."

It is quite alarming that children today are exposed to many concepts that are far beyond their years developmentally. Therein, however, lies a reassuring thought: Any concept that is miles past a child's current level of understanding is pretty much neutralized. Although children may hear adult language—on TV or radio or from peers, older siblings, adult conversations—they will absorb very little conceptually, if anything, beyond the literal words. (Adult-orientated images or experiences, of course, may be much more potent and lasting but will still be understood by the child in a very literal way; fortunately, young children are much more likely to be exposed to age-inappropriate words than images or behaviors.)

What children will absorb is *our reaction* to what they've heard or repeated to us. Like the kindergarten teacher, we'll do well to hold our reactions in check until we've gotten a handle on the *child's* perspective. Should he or she press us about the meaning of a particular word or phrase (during the Clinton scandal more than a few parents of five- and six-year-olds lived through the singularly mortifying experience of being asked to explain the meaning of the phrase "oral sex"), there's no need to panic or go into any kind of detailed explanation. Usually, a calm, very general response— "that's a grownup thing that doesn't really have anything to do with children"—will do the trick.

Sometimes parents find themselves in a situation where young children have heard or been told more than a vague phrase or two about an explicit sexual topic; some age-mate or older sibling or cousin may have taken it upon herself to "show off" by describing a particular sexual act or concept in graphic terms. Though certainly that might make us angry and upset, especially if our child has been confused or upset by the conversation, it's important to remember that in most cases a calm response on our part is always the best. If we can put the incident in a reassuring context—"Oh, sometimes kids like to show off by talking about things that make people mad or grossed out"—it will likely soon be forgotten.

Scary subjects, like AIDS, are another source of concern for parents. Usually when young children ask a question, like "What is AIDS?" they are not looking for any kind of detailed explanation. Probably they've heard the word in passing and are checking it out—in which case you can simply say, "AIDS is a kind of sickness." Sometimes children hear about AIDS (or another scary topic) in a context where people sound sad, upset, or worried. In that case, the child is likely asking for *reassurance*, not *information*, because he may be worried that he or someone else may also get sick. In that case, here's a good way to provide it: "AIDS is a sickness that is very serious. That's why people sound sad when they talk about it. But, Daddy and I know how to keep ourselves safe, and when you get older we'll teach you what you need to know, too."

Gender Roles: Girls Aren't from Venus, Boys Aren't from Mars

As they become more and more aware of the world around them, young children quickly learn that there's much more to the differences between boys and girls and men and women than a few obvious features of anatomy and physiology. Once they're tuned into what's what and who's who, they consciously and unconsciously begin the powerful processes of identification and modeling described earlier. For many parents today who want to avoid the constraints imposed by unhealthy masculine and feminine stereotyping, nurturing an open-minded attitude toward gender roles is an ongoing challenge.

As discussed in Chapter 2, it is impossible to unravel the complex interplay between nature and nurture and how they individually and collectively influence the development of masculinity and femininity in young children. What we do know about these complex processes is: (1) Boys and girls come into the world with some average fundamental differences in certain abilities, but these differences are relatively minor statistically; (2) boys' and girls' brains are exposed to very different sex hormones during much of the prenatal period, with undetermined but likely significant effects; (3) regardless of genetic differences and prenatal conditions, there are a multitude of cultural factors at work from birth on that profoundly influence and shape how boys and girls come to define what it means to be male or female.

We are all aware, of course, of the most obvious examples of these social and cultural influences: name choice, birth announcements, clothing, room decoration and color, and gift and toy selection. These obvious examples, however, tell only a small part of the story. Research has identified much more subtle and powerful ways in which babies are treated differently according to gender. For example, girls when held are placed closer to the body than boys and are spoken to more often and in softer tones. Baby boys, on the other hand, are more often encouraged to engage in active play (like reaching for an object), whereas girls are more often encouraged to engage in verbal play. Once again, these patterns may reflect a chicken-and-egg phenomenon: It is certainly possible that inborn differences are perceived subconsciously by adults, who then, without realizing it, respond with behaviors that reinforce and thereby enlarge them. As T. Berry Brazelton writes in *Toddlers and Parents*, "even in these days when we are consciously trying not to reinforce stereotyped sex roles which may not be productive for the child's future, it is virtually impossible not to treat boys and girls differently."

That said, we can train ourselves to become more sensitized, self-aware, and proactive about many of the choices we make that will send important and lasting messages to our children about gender. As most adults will probably agree, gender roles—both in the workplace and in domestic life—are becoming increasingly fluid. Whereas previously, in fact throughout most of human history, biology truly was considered destiny in terms of the roles that men and women enacted in the world, today these roles are increasingly considered interchangeable. In the society that our children will inherit, we can presume this trend will only continue to grow. We will serve our children best in their formative years by encouraging them to be flexible and creative in their thinking about "proper" masculine and feminine roles.

How does this approach translate to life with a very young child? First, we can explore our own attitudes and values and how we express them, in our words and our behavior. We can continually remind ourselves that girls and boys really aren't from different planets or species and that males and females aren't really "opposite" (sexes): All people are humans who are much more the same than "different." We can also take care not to verbally label aspects of life—hobbies, interests, toys, games, sports, clothes, emotions, styles of relating, personality traits, and the like—as "boy things" or "girl things." Instead, we can let our children know that while they'll notice for sure that boys and girls tend to gravitate toward certain interests and behaviors—and sometimes even make fun of others who display different kinds of interests or behaviors—these patterns are not written in cement anywhere: It's okay for everybody to want to do and be everything and anything.

Notions about gender roles are deeply ingrained in our culture, and it's unrealistic to think that boys and girls won't continue to be socialized and channeled—by peers, adults, merchandisers, and media—in very different directions in the foreseeable future (no matter how consciously nonsexist parents attempt to be). We can certainly help both boys and girls understand, though, that there is a great deal of choice and individuality open to them in expressing themselves—if not so much now, perhaps, definitely as they grow up—regardless of their gender. It might be hard to buck the trend, but we can teach them that, though sometimes they'll choose not to risk it, they always have a choice. This underlying belief system will help engender an underlying attitude of flexibility. It will also take some of the pressure off, by encouraging them to pursue whatever roles and interests they find most appealing and to experiment at least some of the times with those they might otherwise discount and dismiss out of hand.

A much smaller number of parents have an opposite concern: They worry that their child seems intent on near total *rejection* of traditional gender roles—little girls who absolutely refuse to wear dresses and want to play rough games with the boys, little boys who persist in wanting to play with dolls and other "girly" things. More than likely, these children are merely attempting to find and express their own unique style and are strong and independent enough to go against the pack. Their behavior doesn't necessarily "mean" anything about their future gender identity or sexual orientation, as parents might wonder. (If particular children older than five eventually begin to protest regularly that they are not *really* the gender that matches their anatomy or continually say they *hate* the gender they are, consultation with a professional experienced in working with gender issues might be indicated.)

Sexual Orientation: Explaining the Seeming Hard-to-Explain

As we pointed out earlier, sometimes when we're tempted to say, "You're not old enough to know that," what we really mean is that we can't figure out how to explain it, especially to someone so young. Often a topic seems so totally out of the context of a child's life that we just can't seem to come up with a proper starting place.

The topic of homosexuality is a clear example. Sometimes, because they have close family members or friends who are gay, parents want to inform their children—even children as young as five or six—but can't imagine how or when that might be appropriate. Usually their stumbling block is that they're thinking of being lesbian or gay as a purely sexual concept and therefore one that is, or should be kept, totally foreign to the child's world. Here's the key in situations like this: Think of a related issue with which the child is already familiar and start there.

In this case, the concept of *coupling*, which children as young as five or six can certainly understand, is a perfect one. The parent can say something like: "I know you've noticed that when people get older they become attracted to and want to become a romantic couple with someone who is very special to them—like me and Mommy, and Aunt Jane and Uncle Richie, and Jack and his girlfriend, Sara. And I'm sure you've also noticed that all the couples you've met so far are male and female. Well, what you may not know is that some people are attracted to and want to become a couple with someone of the same gender, and that's called being 'gay.' In fact, Mom's friend Sally (or cousin Jim, or Lindsay's mom whom you met at school) is gay, and we want you to know what that means."

Media: "Where Did You Learn to Kiss Like *That*?"

When one of my sons was about three, he almost took my breath away with shock and surprise. He came right over to me one evening totally out of the blue and planted a kiss on my lips that was every bit as passionate (but, thankfully, nowhere near as long) as that famous on-camera smooch Al Gore gave his wife, Tipper, at the 2000 Democratic Convention.

"Where *on earth* did you learn to kiss like that?" I asked, when I was finally able to find my voice.

"On the 'Fornbergs,' Mommy!"

And then I remembered. We had been visiting some relatives recently and the made-for-TV movie *The Thornbirds* was on when we first came in. It happened to be the part where Ralph and Meggie were thrashing around under the covers. Even though there was practically no "skin" of any kind showing (this was the early eighties), my son just knew that something pretty fascinating and important was going on under there. I had noticed that his little nose was practically glued to the screen by the time we were ready to go to the table for dinner.

Young children are paying attention to everything everywhere. Unfortunately, more and more of "everywhere" in the United States—television, the Internet, radio, lyrics, videos, movies, magazines, newspapers, shop windows, advertisements, billboards—is increasingly a high-gloss, high-tech showcase for merchandizing either sex or something else *using* sex. Parents can be vigilant about screening material to which young children are exposed, but truthfully, total censorship is absolutely impossible. When parents tell me confidently, "Oh, we don't even *own* a television!" I always ask, "But I'll bet you've been to the supermarket with your child recently. Have you taken a close look at the text and images on the covers of the women's magazines, especially the ones right there at his eye level, while you're standing there waiting for the line to move up?" Unless we're noticing how and what they're noticing ("That woman in the picture is showing off her breasts to get people's attention. I can see that she caught your attention, too!"), we can't be there to guide them.

Frankly, I'm less concerned with the increasing explicitness of the sexual language and imagery depicted in the public domain than with the sheer volume of it. (The number of sexual references on TV alone *tripled* in the 1990s.) I often encourage parents to think of children as little Martians who've suddenly landed in the midst of North American culture and are trying to make sense of it without the benefit of language or context. With sex referenced at every turn, why wouldn't they look around and conclude that it is singularly glamorous and captivating, absolutely essential to success and happiness—the virtual end all and be all of life itself. Glorified and at the same time trivialized beyond all recognition by the excesses of commercialism, sex in the media, sadly, has lost any semblance of its real meaning.

All the more reason for parents to take a proactive rather than the more typically reactive role in their children's sexual education. (Unfortunately, I am doubtful that the number of adults *available and willing to interpret* media messages for children tripled as well during the nineties.) The values that most parents want their children to hold dear about gender, sexuality, and relationships are the opposite of the shallow, distorted, and manipulative ones to which they will be constantly and shamelessly exposed.

The good news is that parents are at the center of their children's universe, the translators of their immediate experience, and the primary source of their baseline values. If we are able to look honestly at the world of sexuality through our children's eyes and communicate about it with them directly, we can provide the kind of wholesome and healthful lens children will need to evaluate incoming sexual messages and images correctly, perhaps for a lifetime. That's very good news, indeed.

6

Parents and Preschools as Partners

In important respects, the worlds of the family, the day care provider, and the preschool are—or should be—seamlessly connected. Because children at this tender age are still relatively dependent and vulnerable, they require uniquely child-centered environments organized around the distinctive physical, social, emotional, and intellectual needs and characteristics of early childhood. All of the sights, sounds, smells, and textures that greet children as they enter these environments should say the same thing: "Welcome! This space is different from all others. It is specially created for *you*."

Almost everything that has been said in this book so far can and, in my mind, should be applied to early childhood settings outside the home. Young children, as we have said, are constantly in the process of learning about themselves and the world around them, as an organic by-product of living, experiencing, and relating. Sexual learning is no different: Though some of what young children learn about sexuality is "taught" directly through instruction, most of their attitudes and understandings are "caught" incidentally through experience. Therefore, the conditions of sexual learning first discussed in Chapter 2 apply to *all* environments, and especially to those that cater directly to the needs of the young child.

This chapter is written for parents and also for staff who work in early childhood settings so that all of us can find ourselves on the "same page" in understanding and meeting the needs of young children. It's intended to provide a very general blueprint for creating and/or assessing the sexuality component of early childhood programs. You may want to share this chapter with your children's providers or teachers (or vice versa) as a way of beginning a dialogue about the possibilities open to early childhood settings.

Creating Positive Conditions for Learning

Like parents, many early-childhood care providers are committed to maximizing the conditions for healthy sexual learning in their schools and centers. Also like parents, they will probably need to begin this process by educating and reeducating themselves and their staffs. As a first step, they'll want to consider many of the principles laid out in the early chapters of this book:

- "Sexuality education" is vastly different from traditional notions of "sex education"; it encompasses complex issues of *identity, development, sensuality, intimacy, values,* and *health.*
- *Gender,* not sex, comprises the largest component of who we are as sexual people.
- Sexual learning occurs from birth on; most sexual learning occurs through daily living experiences, not direct teaching.
- All children from birth through adolescence have five developmental needs in relation to sexuality: *affirmation, information, values clarification, limit setting,* and *anticipatory guidance*; in large measure, our children's sexual health depends on how skillfully adults are able to recognize, understand, and respond to these universal needs.
- Children are our best teachers and will help us know what they need to learn.

- Families and schools are partners in meeting sexual education needs.

Just as they attend proactively to other fundamental needs of children in their care, providers will need to organize the living and learning environment in their facilities in ways that best meet the sexual education needs of their young charges. To be successful, they'll need to take four important steps: making sexuality education a priority, developing institutional policies, educating and engaging parents, and training staff.

Why Make Sexuality a Priority in Early Childhood Settings?

Parents are the first and most important sexuality educators in a child's life. What they teach, especially what they teach through daily reactions and interactions, provides the foundation for all later learning—whether they are aware of it or not. (Even avoidance of the subject of sexuality altogether teaches a powerful and lasting lesson!) Parents, then, really have no choice about whether to take on their role as sexuality educators: Your role is inevitable, and your only choices are how proactively and skillfully you will take it on and how positive and developmentally supportive the messages you deliver about sexuality will be.

Much the same can be said about the staff in early childhood programs. Teachers of young children, too, are involved inevitably in the sexual learning process; they are literally surrounded by children who are bursting with curiosity about themselves, their bodies, their origins, and what it means to be a girl or boy, and who are constantly taking in formative knowledge about values, health, and relationships. Every single day, children *bring in* to early childhood settings the same kinds of needs, questions, and situations we've been discussing throughout this book—and they *take away* important information about the immediate adults in their lives and how comfortable and reliable they are as sources of encouragement, support, and knowledge.

Tragically, because of adult avoidance, fear, confusion, and discomfort, most children do not come to see the immediate grownups in their lives as reliable or available mentors about sexuality—including their teachers. No wonder that by the early elementary school years, sex has often become the favored centerpiece of covert conversations on playgrounds, in bathrooms, and on school buses, purposefully away from the eyes and ears of adults. This near universal pattern means that, by the age of seven or eight, many children have already concluded that they will have to look to each other for the answers to their questions and for validation that their curiosity is normal and acceptable. It also means they've learned to think of sexuality as different and apart from the rest of life—that they are to treat it, talk about it, think about, and learn about it differently from all other subjects. That belief in itself is perhaps the most damaging of all to their later ability to integrate sexuality healthfully into their lives.

Even in the healthiest of social and cultural contexts, parents and teachers need to be seen as reliable resources about all subjects, including sexuality. In twenty-first-century America their ready availability has become an absolute necessity. Everyone who knows and cares about children and their fundamental needs is concerned about the toxicity of American culture for impressionable children and adolescents. The pervasiveness of exploitative sexual messages and imagery in the media and the increasing and shameless targeting of younger and younger children by entertainers and merchandisers are working in tandem to plunge powerful "youth culture" values and ideals downward even into the elementary school years.

In the midst of this onslaught, parents and schools must face a hard reality: *We may have no one to blame but ourselves.* To a large degree these unsavory forces in popular culture are simply attempting to take advantage of the vacuum that we ourselves have created in children's lives about sexuality with our own silence and evasion.

As worried as I am about these trends and how vulnerable our children may be to their effects, I am equally convinced that we parents and teachers are in a strong position to neutralize the problem *almost entirely* by taking on our rightful and proper roles in sexuality education. (In my elementary and middle- and high-school classes, I can easily spot children and adolescents, usually within minutes, who've been raised in families where sexuality is treated openly and directly; they are the kids who are the least embarrassed and also the most savvy about negative influences like those in the media.) And, if we in fact intend to become an effective counterweight to the winds of popular culture, we'll need to establish ourselves *as early as possible* as credible sources of affirmation, information, values, limits, and guidance.

Families and schools can be vital partners in shaping a young child's present experience and future decisions. Teachers, like parents, are powerful role models. They help determine children's feelings about themselves and their ability to make caring, responsible, and informed choices. They are also important resources in helping to protect children from exploitation and abuse. Families and schools, especially if they work consciously and proactively together, can become effective buffers against an aggressive, unbridled popular culture. In fact, forging partnerships between schools and families around issues like sexuality is not a luxury but an absolute necessity in today's world.

Principles, Goals, and Practices

Making sexuality education a priority is a crucial first step in meeting children's needs in early childhood facilities and in creating working partnerships with parents. However, because sexuality is a complex, sensitive, potentially controversial issue, enthusiasm and good intentions will need to be combined with a methodical approach for setting policies, identifying goals, and implementing sound practices.

The Center for Family Life Education in Hackensack, New Jersey, has been a leader for over a decade in the field of early childhood sexuality education. Educators at the center have created a number of excellent materials and workshops for enabling early childhood facilities to examine their programs carefully and to maximize the conditions for healthy sexual learning. The center's work with teachers and administrators begins with helping staff think about and develop their own underlying philosophy, first to give their work a firm base and then to guide them in formulating specific goals and practices. Below is a sample statement that many facilities working with the center have used as a starting place in creating their own policies. Its eloquence and simplicity are at the same time enlightening and reassuring in that both parents and teachers begin to think about the appropriate roles of early childhood facilities in healthy sexual development.

A Philosophy for Young People's Learning about Sexuality
    1. We believe that sexuality:
        a. Is a positive and fundamental part of human existence and affects all aspects of our lives.
        b. Is basic to who we are as male or female persons.
        c. Is a natural part of us from birth to death.
    2. We believe that children:
        a. Begin learning about sexuality as soon as they are born and will continue to learn throughout their lives.
        b. Learn about sexuality through their interactions with the total environment.
        c. Learn from how people touch them, talk with them, and expect them to behave as male or female.

   d. Learn attitudes and values about sexuality that affect
      future feelings and behaviors.
   e. Are naturally curious about how their bodies look and
      work, about how male and female bodies differ, and
      about where babies come from.
   f. Trust and communicate with adults who are open and
      honest with them.
   g. Are more vulnerable to exploitation and abuse when they
      do not have age-appropriate information about sexuality.
3. We believe that parents are their children's most important teachers.
4. We believe that early childhood staff can be a positive
   influence in children's sexual learning, assisting parents in
   their role as their child's most important caregiver and
   teacher.

Goals and Practices

Once basic principles have been identified, early childhood
providers need to set specific learning goals for the children in their
care. These concepts should be clear and direct: "Children will
learn that it is okay to be curious about sexuality and ask questions
about it." "Children will develop positive feelings about their bodies and learn to use correct words for all of their body parts and
their functions." "Children will feel good about being a girl or a
boy and experience a full range of choices open to them regardless
of their gender." "Children will begin to understand the difference
between public and private behaviors."

Next, administrators and staff will need to translate their goals
into concrete strategies and practices. A good way to begin is by
identifying day-to-day situations relating to sexuality that are common to all early childhood settings and then working together to
identify healthy responses. Some examples:

- What rules will adults follow in encouraging appropriate and nurturing touch among children and staff? How about touching—and looking—that occurs between children? Under what circumstances will it be considered acceptable and not?
- How and where will diapering occur? Will children be allowed (or encouraged) to watch? What rules will be in place regarding bathroom facilities (separate or mixed genders; doors open or closed)? Regarding how staff will assist in toileting or potty training? How about nudity? Will children be allowed to change and toilet together? How will staff respond to children who ask for privacy while toileting or changing?
- What will be the reaction if children engage in "toilet talk" or use slang or "babyish" terms? How will staff respond to children's questions about their origins and about body differences? Will there be a specific curriculum designed to help children learn about their bodies, including the sexual parts and their functions?
- What should be the reaction to masturbation—in relatively public and/or private spaces? What if children are playing "doctor" or examining each other in the bathroom? What guidelines will be used to determine if a child's sexuality-related activity indicates an underlying emotional problem or the possibility of abuse?

Staff will also want to think through the complex and important issue of gender roles. They'll need to identify strategies for assuring that boys and girls experience equitable treatment and encouragement during both free play and structured activities. They'll want to examine their own personal use of language (*policeman, fireman, mailman* versus *police officer, firefighter, mail carrier*), as well as the range of books, songs, toys, videos, and games available in the facility, to assure that the prevailing gender messages are fundamentally nonsexist and to provide a balance of male and female adult role models. They'll also want to scrutinize less obvious situations in which boys and girls commonly receive more subtle, yet powerful, discriminatory treatment. For example, teachers (and parents) tend to give praise or criticism and to respond to specific kinds of emotions or problematic behavior differently according to gender. (Research demonstrates that boys, because they tend to be more active, often receive more reprimands than girls, whereas girls receive more positive reinforcement when they express "soft" emotions like fear but are discouraged more often than boys from expressing anger or aggression.) Finally, it will be important for staff to examine personal and professional reactions to children who frequently engage in "cross-gender" behaviors—for example, boys who consistently like to play dress-up and girls who gravitate to physically aggressive games—or children who "resist" trying out nonstereotypical play activities.

Increasingly, as homosexuality becomes more of an accepted fact of life in American society, families headed by gay couples are becoming much more visible in school communities and elsewhere. These parents, like all parents, want their children to feel comfortable, accepted, and included, even though they may be the only ones in their group who have "two moms" or "two dads"; their children, like all children, will need and want to be able to share freely about family activities, incidental and important—and about the people in their lives whom they love and count on the most—without experiencing disapproval or ridicule. Determining how best to educate and sensitize staff, as well as the children in their care and the children's families, about the great variety of family structures common to modern life—and to their school or facility—is another essential area for discussion.

While it's difficult if not impossible and even counterproductive to dictate hard-and-fast rules to early childhood teachers and staff in handling day-to-day circumstances, a steadfast commitment to ongoing dialogue about these issues is what's really important.

With a clear philosophy and an in-depth understanding of developmental needs in place and a good measure of self awareness, capable educators, as I always tell them, simply can't go too far wrong in their responses!

Educating and Engaging Parents

Very often, what prevents early childhood facilities from taking proactive steps to establish these kinds of overt policies and practices is the fear of negative parental reaction or even reprisal. In the wake of several widely publicized child sexual abuse scandals in the 1980s (about which many of the allegations have since been discredited), many preschool and other early childhood personnel have remained understandably leery of being perceived as or accused of "sexualizing" young children in any way. Sadly, many shy away even from providing the wholly appropriate physical touch and hugs that young children need every bit as much as their minimum daily requirements for nutrition, stimulation, activity, playmates, punch, cookies, and naptime.

Much of this book to this point is devoted to defining what it means to be a sexual person "from birth on" and explaining the multiple ways in which infants and young children learn continually—in the course of daily living—about themselves and others as sexual and gendered people. Adults who attempt to support and nourish those learning processes in healthy ways *are not in any way* "sexualizing" young children. To "sexualize" a child or adolescent means something quite the opposite: It is an attempt to turn a young person into a sexual object for one's own selfish purposes. Nor does sexuality education in schools "sexualize"—or bring sexuality into—a school environment in an unnatural or inappropriate way; its purpose is to meet children *where they already are,* as growing sexual people and to support their natural, ongoing development in positive and healthy ways.

Ironically, when we avoid dealing with sexual issues directly and proactively in preschool environments, we actually make our children *more* vulnerable, not less. By skipping over important steps in their normal developmental and educational timetable, we make it harder for them to learn more sophisticated concepts later on. Moreover, *our* avoidance will eventually cause *them* to avoid *us* and to discount us as reliable resources; *our* discomfort will cause *them* discomfort, and those feelings eventually may become a serious learning and communication barrier. Finally, if children have no clear vocabulary for or practice in talking about the sexual parts of their bodies and if, in fact, adults have directly or indirectly discouraged them from talking about sexuality at all, they will be *more* vulnerable to truly abusive situations and *less* able to ask for the help they may need.

We serve children best when we are careful not to be afraid of the wrong things. Most important, parents and teachers need to learn not to fear one another. Parents should be able to rely on schools to reinforce the healthy messages about sexuality that they give at home; teachers should be able to count on parents to support their efforts in school as they attempt to meet clear developmental needs. We *can* learn to speak the same language and understand the same concepts about childhood sexuality and early sexual learning. Either parents or schools can initiate the dialogue, and then everyone can work together to arrive at the right kinds of principles, goals, and practices that will best meet our children's needs.

Preparing and Training Staff

Teachers and other staff members working in early childhood settings may need special help in learning how to address the issue of sexuality in positive and developmentally appropriate ways. Many if not most educators may have had no specialized training in sexuality as part of their professional development; what others have received may not be at all adequate. Many have come to adulthood with educational gaps in their own formal sexual learning and with misplaced anxieties about providing "too much information too soon." Few experienced the kinds of adult role models as they were growing up—and certainly even fewer at the early childhood level!—who demonstrated what an adult looks and sounds like when he or she is talking openly and comfortably with a young person about sexuality. And some will be just plain embarrassed about the whole subject altogether. In short, early childhood educators are a lot like parents (and most other adults in the United States)!

What early childhood personnel *do* have is an uncanny ability to "read" children and to empathize with their immediate moods, feelings, and needs. By virtue of the intimate and nurturing environments in which they work and the carefully honed teaching and interpersonal skills they must cultivate, early childhood educators are often exquisitely attuned to the thoughts, questions, reactions, and intellectual capabilities of young children. They also have seemingly boundless energy, are enormously flexible, and possess an unshakable commitment to meeting real developmental needs. With the right kind of encouragement, support, and information—and opportunities to work through their own residual discomfort or anxieties—with very few exceptions I find they are a natural and excellent "fit" for the role of sexuality educator.

One good approach in preparing staff is to introduce them to the five-needs paradigm first described in Chapter 1. The paradigm is based on the observation that whenever children present us with sexual issues or situations—regardless of their age—they are always expressing one or more of the following easily identifiable, developmentally based needs:

Affirmation: Children need parents and teachers to recognize and validate their particular stage of sexual development.

Information giving: Children need factual knowledge and concepts about sexuality, presented in ongoing and age-appropriate ways.

Values clarification: Children need parents and teachers to help shape positive, healthy attitudes and values about sexuality, and as children become more socially aware, they need parents and teachers to clarify and interpret competing values and values systems in the surrounding culture.

Limit setting: Children need parents and teachers to create a healthy and safe environment by stating and reinforcing age-appropriate rules and limits.

Anticipatory guidance: Children need parents and teachers to help them learn how to avoid or handle potentially harmful situations and to prepare them for times when they will need to rely on themselves to make responsible and healthy choices.

For educators, as for parents, the first step in using the five-needs paradigm effectively is to acquire a thorough understanding of each need; the second is to become skilled in recognizing each of the needs as they present themselves; and the third, to develop competence and confidence in matching supportive adult responses to each of the developmental needs. Below are some common examples of how young children may express their developmental needs around sexuality in early childhood settings, matched with some examples of developmentally supportive staff responses.

Affirming Normal Development

Needs. Young children are exceptionally curious about their bodies, about other people's bodies, and about body differences. They express their curiosity verbally and through physical exploration.

Eventually they begin to wonder about their origins and become curious about the processes of reproduction, and they look to parents and other caretakers to provide answers. Children also need to give and receive loving touch from parents and caretakers to feel good about themselves and their bodies and learn about the pleasures and emotional comfort associated with physical affection and closeness.

Responses. Caretakers and teachers need to understand the normal stages and processes of sexual development in early childhood. They need to show acceptance of children's natural interest in learning about their bodies (including the sexual parts and functions) and their origins. Staff also need to understand and affirm that masturbation and sexual play between young children are expressions of normal, healthy curiosity. Also, they'll need to be able to freely give and accept appropriate physical affection.

Giving Information

Needs. Children need correct information about the names and functions of all their body parts. They need to know that their caretakers will respond honestly and in a relaxed and open manner to all questions about the human body—including the sexual parts—and to questions about babies and their origins.

Responses. Teachers and caretakers need to develop skills in becoming "askable" resources. They need to understand that *the way* they respond to children's curiosity will teach every bit as much as *what* they say. They'll need to be able to discern what children really want to know when they ask questions about their bodies or their origins; to give simple, direct, and concrete responses to all questions; and to gently correct misconceptions. They'll also need to know how to assess whether they've adequately satisfied the child's curiosity. Ideally, they'll also provide opportunities for children to learn from their own observations (visits by pregnant women and newborns) and to discover information on their own through resources available in the facility (anatomically correct dolls, "birthing dolls," and books).

Shaping Values

Needs. A young child's values revolve around meeting her or his own immediate needs. It is up to parents and teachers, especially, to help children acquire the attitudes and values they will need to take care of themselves, to be successful in their relationships, and to function independently in the world. One central aspect of sexuality—gender roles and identity—is deeply value-laden for adults. Young children, on the other hand, are open to all possibilities! Girls will want to stand up to urinate and play roughly with the boys; boys will pretend to breastfeed and deliver babies and enjoy wearing ladies' makeup and high heels. Eventually, children will need to conform to a greater or lesser extent to society's gender role expectations, but early childhood is a time for creative experimentation with all kinds of roles and experiences, unrestricted by adult preconceptions or rules.

Responses. Young children learn sexual values constantly from adult role models, who communicate attitudes and values about the human body continually through their body language, tone of voice, facial expression, and physical touch. As gendered people and in the ways they respond consciously and unconsciously to young children's behavior, they are constantly sending messages about "proper" roles for males and females. Becoming as aware as possible of the values they hope to communicate about sex and gender—and taking care not to send messages that are unnecessarily negative or restrictive—will serve children best.

Setting Limits

Needs. Babies and young children have little conception of the boundaries and limitations imposed by the physical and social worlds. Once again, it is up to parents and teachers first to provide safe and healthy limits and eventually to instill them. In relation to sexuality, children eventually will need to learn that there are limits to the ways in which they will be allowed to satisfy their curiosity. For example, they will need to learn that it is inappropriate to touch themselves or others, or to be touched by others, in certain ways and at certain times, just as they will need to learn appropriate rules regarding nudity and privacy.

Responses. Parents and teachers are constantly setting limits around young children's behavior. In regard to sexuality, early childhood settings provide countless "teachable moments" for helping children understand that some parts of the body are to be kept private except under special circumstances; that certain kinds of looking and touching are appropriate and others are not; and that children and adults have both a right to privacy and a right to control how and when they are touched by others. Like parents, teachers and staff will need to learn how best to set and teach limits without making children feel ashamed of their bodies, their curiosity, or their enjoyment, by learning to giving dual-level messages ("I can see that rubbing on your genitals gives you very pleasant feelings. But please remember that you're big enough now to pick more private places to enjoy them.").

Providing Guidance

Needs. As children become increasingly independent, they will face important choices. To better meet their own needs, resolve conflicts with others, and solve their own problems, they will need to learn important communication and decision-making skills. Early childhood environments provide many opportunities in the course of the day to teach children interpersonal and problem-solving skills. Children will benefit when teachers and staff are able to help them apply these skills equally to situations involving sexuality.

Responses. Early childhood staff can help children understand that their behavior can have important positive or negative effects. They can encourage children to develop empathy for the needs and feelings of others and can help them learn to be direct in letting other children (and adults) know how certain behaviors make them feel. In the important area of sexuality, children can be helped to understand that they—and others—have certain rights in relation to their own bodies and certain responsibilities to others in relation to theirs. As staff members observe children toileting, changing clothing, or playing together, they can be alert to situations involving conflict, pressure, or discomfort. They can intervene best not by taking charge but by asking the children to describe very directly what is happening and to talk openly about their feelings and reactions. In this way, without creating unnecessary guilt, shame, or anxiety, they teach children to be respectful and responsive to other people's limits ("I don't like it when you try to peek at my genitals when I'm getting changed.") and to be expressive about their own needs and feelings ("It makes me mad when you point at my penis and laugh. Please stop."). They can also use each experience as a matter-of-fact opportunity to calmly remind children about appropriate rules regarding touch, privacy, or nudity: "In school, we keep our clothes on when we play." "We listen when others tell us not to look at or touch them in certain ways." "We need to let other people know when their behavior makes us feel angry or uncomfortable, and we can always find an adult who will help if we need to."

Thinking About the Unthinkable:
Child Sexual Abuse

When one of my sons was in preschool, we read a children's story-book together about appropriate and inappropriate touch. The book explained that certain parts of the body (the parts we keep covered by a bathing suit) are "private" and that other people should not look at or touch our "private parts" except under very special circumstances. It also gave advice about what children should do if someone tried to make them feel bad, pressured, or uncomfortable in any way about their "private parts."

The book made *me* uncomfortable, but I couldn't quite put my finger on exactly why. I asked my son what he thought the book was trying to teach him about "private parts." Without hesitation, he explained, "Oh—they're trying to teach you that private parts are *very* bad!"

While books and programs that attempt to teach children about "good touches" and "bad touches" no doubt are well intentioned, I have long worried about them. First, I find that, indirectly, they place too much of the onus for preventing sexual abuse on children rather than adults. There is a fine line in a very young child's mind, I fear, between "I can make this stop if I don't like it," and "I'm responsible for fixing this, and if I don't, then I must be responsi-ble for it happening." I also worry about the sex-negative under-tones communicated in any educational process where the funda-mental context is abuse, not healthy sexuality, especially when sex-ual parts ("privates") are not even called directly by name. Moreover, can we really expect young children to distinguish the idea that "having people touch my private parts is bad" from the notion that, therefore, "my sexual parts must be bad"?

Parents and other adults who are responsible for the well-being of young children must recognize first that our most important job in preventing (and reporting) child sexual abuse is to train ourselves, not our children; we are the ones who will need to be vigilant and on guard through adequate supervision of our children's activities and careful screening of those individuals to whose care we entrust our children. We also need to educate ourselves to be able to detect quickly whether, despite our precautions, abuse has occurred and to react calmly and in the most supportive and developmentally appropriate ways we possibly can. (Experts in the field of abuse point out that in the aftermath of the discovery of an abuse situation, the *reactions of others* can strongly influence, if not determine, how well the child is subsequently able to cope and to heal.)

All parents, caretakers, and educators should be alert to the warning signs of possible abuse and should seek immediate advice from a pediatrician or trained specialist if they notice evidence of the following in a preschool or elementary-aged child: unusual discharge from the genitals; compulsive masturbation in public (after the child is old enough to understand the concept of privacy and/or after repeated attempts to discourage the behavior); excessive interest in touching other people or in drawing pictures of genitals; a preoccupation with sex that interferes with friendships or school life; a child's engaging in atypical sex play (such as oral, anal, or vaginal intercourse, or penetration with fingers or objects) with an age-mate; involvement in sex play of *any* kind with a child three or more years older; or appearing fearful, angry, or withdrawn in the presence of a suspected abuser. Any of these activities *might* indicate that a child has been exposed to sexually explicit material or has been sexually abused.

There certainly are helpful and important safety instructions that we should give young children directly about appropriate and inappropriate genital touching. However, to avoid attaching unnecessary and potentially harmful fear, anxiety, or negativity to *sex* or *the genitalia,* these messages need to be communicated within a larger and much more positive context than child sexual-abuse prevention. We should encourage children to talk about *all kinds* of touch they've experienced or might experience—good, bad, confusing, pleasurable, fun, hurtful, or harmful—and make sure they understand their right to determine, in most situations, who can touch them and where, how, or when. (That means we ourselves have to be consistently respectful of their wishes and not insist, for example, that they give us—or other relatives or friends—welcoming or good night kisses or hugs when it's not to their liking.) We'll need to also make clear the specific kinds of safety- or health-related situations in which trusted adults—parents, caretakers, teachers, doctors, nurses, and the like—will need to pick them up or touch them, even when it's *not* to their liking!

In the context of this larger ongoing discussion about touch—and also in talking with children about setting appropriate limits around nudity and privacy—parents and other caretakers can be sure to make certain points that will help protect children against abuse: "It's not okay for an older or bigger person to look at or touch your penis or vulva unless it's for one of the reasons we've talked about." "Tell an adult right away if sometime touches you or wants to touch you in a way that feels even a little bit bad or 'funny' or 'wrong.'" "Adults should never ask a child to keep secrets from their parents or teachers or other family members (unless everyone is planning a fun surprise for someone special!). Come and tell me right away if that happens." "You can *always* tell me about anyone or anything that is bothering or worrying you in any way. I will *always* listen and take care of you." Most important of all is not specifically what parents and other caretakers *say* around these issues but what they *do*. Children at the least risk for abuse are probably those who are nurtured by adults who can consistently do the following: show respect for children's physical space and privacy and expect them to respect others'; teach them directly about *healthy* sexuality and thereby enable them to detect clearly what is *un*healthy; model and teach respect and positive regard for the sexual parts of the human body; and demonstrate that they will listen to and trust a child's feelings and perceptions, no matter what.

Schools can also help insure that abuse prevention messages avoid promoting unnecessary guilt or negativity, by making sure that children receive them in the context of an ongoing, positive, and holistic approach to dealing with the entire subject of sexuality and normal sexual development. (I remember a time in the 1980s when elementary-aged students across the country commonly received two—and only two—kinds of "sexuality" education in school: AIDS education and child sexual abuse–prevention training.) Health-affirming and age-appropriate sexuality education is *not* about "damage control." It *is* about nurturing and supporting healthy growth and development in all of the ways we've been discussing throughout this book.

One last comment (and a personal pet peeve) about the phrase *private parts*. I think it best that we not label any body parts as "private" *or* "public." Every human being has many different kinds of body organs. They are all "parts," period. Deciding whether and when we should keep them private or allow them to be seen or touched, involves a complex set of personal, interpersonal, social, cultural—sometimes even subcultural—rules and expectations. (When I go to the Orthodox Jewish wedding of the son of a friend in a few months, I will keep my arms fully covered because that is the custom for Jewish women under those circumstances. Will that make my arms "private parts"?) We confuse children, especially young children, when we label our parts instead of our circumstances; and, when we label certain parts as fundamentally *different* by placing them in a unique linguistic category, we risk their being seen in some way as fundamentally *negative* or *separate*. It may seem like splitting hairs, but I'd suggest that whenever we talk to children about sexual parts, we uniformly call them genitals, or penises or vulvas, or testicles or scrotums or vaginas—and that we talk about *when it is appropriate to keep them* private rather than calling them *privates*.

7

It Should Be Elementary: Sex Education and Primary Schools

A few years ago, I was invited to teach a program to the entire fifth grade at a large public elementary school. It happened to be a school where I had worked with parents for many years, and I felt honored when they asked me to spend time with their children.

Then the vice-principal called to prep me for the program. "We're really very glad you're coming," she explained, "but we need to let you know that while you are here in the building, there are three words you can't say."

"Okay," I said as I braced myself. "Let's have them."

"The words you can't say are *intercourse, fertilization,* and, of course, *sex.*"

"I can't even say the word *sex?* But I'm The Sex Lady. That's what all the kids usually call me. Heck, that's what their *parents* call me!"

"We're sorry," the woman said, "but the county guidelines are very clear. The fifth grade program is about puberty, adolescence, growing up, wet dreams, and periods—period. We're not allowed to change or add anything at all."

"So I *can* mention sperm and eggs, and penises and vaginas, right? I just *can't* talk about how the two get together, as in fertilization, or sex, or intercourse?"

"Right."

"But I know these are bright kids, and it's a very big class. Surely one student or another will wonder how on earth the sperm and egg come together to create a new life, and they'll think to ask me a question about it."

"In a case like that," the vice-principal said, "there are a couple of things you can do. You can say that that is not a topic we are permitted to discuss in this grade [teachers can answer questions about sex, intercourse, or fertilization later in sixth grade, she told me, but they can't bring up the concepts directly until eighth grade.] Then you can encourage the student to go home and ask her or his parent about the information they want."

"I'm really sorry, but I don't think I can take on this teaching assignment," I said. "As an educator, I just don't think I can put myself in a position where I might have to tell a child that a perfectly intelligent, honest, and developmentally right-on question can't be asked and answered in a school building. After all, these are questions that *six-year-olds* are known to ask, let alone sixth graders! No matter what else I might try to teach them, that's what I'm afraid they'll remember.

"Most of all, I don't want them to think that the immediate and most trusted adults in their lives—including, and especially, their teachers—aren't available to them for teaching."

The compromise the school came up with was a good one. A letter went home saying that a guest speaker would be at school expressly to review and directly support the approved fifth-grade curriculum *and* that students would be free to bring up additional or related topics or questions for discussion or clarification, even those not specifically designated in the curriculum. Any parent who did not wish his or her child to participate was free to ask that the child be excused (none did). The letter went on to say, "Our children are growing up and entering a complex and confusing world. We want to do as much as we possibly can to prepare them before they leave us and go off to middle school. We hope you will encourage your child to participate."

Why Are Schools So Out of Touch?

The subject of sex is still taboo in many schools in the United States. Teachers across the country are often reluctant about—and in many cases prohibited from—broaching subjects related to sexuality or creating learning environments that are welcoming to children's questions. The emotionally and politically charged nature of sexuality education in the United States, even for students in the older grades, has made teachers and administrators increasingly skittish about tackling what is perceived to be highly controversial and potentially explosive subject matter. Just the *possibility* of negative parental or community backlash is enough to cause apprehensive educators and administrators to "back burner" the topic indefinitely.

Our children pay a heavy price for this abdication of adult responsibility. Our job as teachers and parents is to prepare children and adolescents to live in the world as it is, not as we might like it to be. Today's world is one in which many children begin to experience pubertal changes as early as eight. It's one in which millions of teenagers each year experience pregnancies and sexually transmitted infections. And it's one in which *all* children and adolescents are bombarded with thousands upon thousands of messages and images in advertising and the entertainment media that teach distorted values and invite precocious, unhealthy behaviors.

Our current strategy—keeping our children "sheltered" and ignorant—is false protection. It is those children who are knowledgeable about their bodies and about healthy sexuality and who receive permission and encouragement to discuss these topics with adults *at any time and at any age* who are best equipped to deal with them. And it's just plain common sense that parents and teachers need to establish a strong foundation for learning in the early grades. Young children should learn about sexuality as they do all other subjects, starting first with simple vocabulary and content and gradually moving on to more complex ideas and concepts. Ann Schurmann, author of several important publications on elementary education, puts it clearly: The idea of evading questions or telling children fictions when they are young and then arbitrarily introducing the complexities of the body and sex all at once in middle or high school is as illogical as telling them myths about math until fifth grade and then suddenly jumping into long division.

It will be hard for us to catch up. Not only among educators but throughout American culture, there exists widespread ignorance of the developmentally appropriate sexuality-education needs of young children—particularly in school-based settings. Where sexuality education occurs at all, the grade levels targeted are most often grades five and above, and even then many subjects are "off limits." As a result, even seasoned teachers and administrators must often find it *nearly impossible* to imagine what such a program might look like for the youngest of students. I've written this chapter to help parents and teachers begin to do just that—to envision wonderful and exciting possibilities for meaningful, age-appropriate education in the early grades.

Imagining—and Creating— Programs for Young Children

Not long ago I worked with a small group of kindergarten and first-grade teachers to help them "imagine" how an early childhood health and sexuality program might take shape in their classrooms. At the time, they were part of a larger team of teachers working on revamping and enriching their school's early-childhood science curriculum. The teachers involved—all from the same private, coed, K–12 school—spent several weeks during the summer months examining the ways in which young children naturally think about and explore their immediate and surrounding worlds, including how they think and learn about their own bodies.

In U.S. schools, information related to sexuality is taught within a variety of contexts and subject matters, such as health, social studies, science, home economics, and, most often, "family life education." At this particular school, it was determined that health education, already taught in middle and high grades as applied science, was the most appropriate context for sexuality education. Part of the teachers' charge during the summer workshop, therefore, was to consider the following questions: (1) What are the direct connections between science content and health content and how can early childhood teachers best interconnect these subjects for their students? (2) What is the common core of learning that will contribute to the health literacy of early childhood learners?

In searching for answers, the teachers began by consulting works written by leading thinkers in the fields of health, science, early childhood, and sexuality education. After much exploration and discussion, they reached the conclusion that the common core of learning in health for early childhood students should ideally include the following ten topics:

1. Living things and how they are sustained
2. Diversity in nature and among individuals, families, and cultures
3. Human development and the human life cycle
4. Body parts, functions, and systems
5. Personal health and disease prevention
6. Mental health and coping with change
7. Communication, decision-making, and problem-solving skills

8. Group behavior and resolving conflicts
9. Cultural influences on health behaviors
10. Interdependence with the environment

In addition, the teachers also adopted the philosophical statements about early childhood sexual learning listed in Chapter 6 (see page 116), finding them to be a good and natural fit for their own school community.

But What If Parents Object?

Having committed themselves to expanding and improving the school's program, the teachers were at once excited and very nervous. As the discussion moved along from the theoretical ("This makes such good sense for all of our students!") to the practical ("Oh dear, do we really think we can we pull this off?"), they began to raise significant considerations and worries about the prospects of implementing a health and sexuality curriculum in the lower grades. These anxieties were deeply felt, and—to no one's surprise—centered primarily on the sexuality component of the program. Foremost on the minds of all of the teachers was the potential for negative reactions from parents. Teachers worried whether parents would accept the idea that sexuality content material was in fact developmentally appropriate for their four-through six-year-old children. And even so, what if parents themselves wanted to be the ones to deliver this information to their children? Wouldn't a school-based program at this age be considered an unwelcome intrusion into their parental role? What if some children in a given class were developmentally ready for this information but others were not? How would the teacher be able to reassure the parents of all children about the appropriateness of the program, and how could the program proceed if that were not possible?

Fortunately, throughout the course of the project, teachers are able to revisit their concerns as often as necessary to work them through to a mutually comfortable and acceptable resolution. Eventually, through several segments of ongoing dialogue, they finally were able to recognize and face the real source of their reluctance: It was actually their *own* internal discomfort or lack of confidence in *this* material for *this* age group that was getting in their way.

With this breakthrough, the teachers became acutely aware of their own *mis*education and *under*education concerning childhood sexuality. They were suddenly hungry for information about the developmental learning needs of four- through six-year-olds. Through readings, presentations, and group discussion, they gradually began to understand and integrate many of the central concepts in this book: (1) that human sexuality is an aspect of one's total identity and a concept infinitely broader than the topics of genital sex and reproduction; (2) that sexual learning and development are ongoing, lifelong processes that occur automatically and primarily nonverbally through daily life experiences; and (3) that a young child's earliest questions about sex and reproduction result from an internal timetable and are normal, predictable, and sequenced according to the level of his or her cognitive development.

Teachers came away from these discussions with much of the confidence and reassurance they needed. They no longer saw themselves as potentially "putting ideas" in children's minds before they were ready to have them. When children ask a question, they concluded, it is always *age*-appropriate for them to receive an answer; for same-age children who haven't yet thought to ask, it is still *stage*-appropriate for them to be within earshot. Teachers also stopped worrying about their work being fundamentally at cross-purposes with the role of parents. Since, as they came to understand, sexuality education occurs constantly from birth on, all adults in a child's life automatically do take part; the only choice is how proactively they do so. Though families and schools perform different kinds of functions in this process because they are different kinds of institutions, these roles are not mutually exclusive but complementary and entwined. Opening up dialogue about what is happening in school only serves to encourage teachers and parents to work together proactively to identify and dovetail their respective roles.

A Prism for Studying Life Itself

These discussions also opened teachers' minds to a broadened understanding of the subject of human sexuality and, in turn, to a multitude of related curricular possibilities. Once enlarged beyond the narrow, often sensationalized and anxiety-provoking subject of "sex," the topic of sexuality becomes a veritable prism for studying life itself: human growth and development, pregnancy and fetal development, body functions and systems, life stages and cycles, gender roles and relationships, family life, intimacy, emotions, self-esteem, self- and body image, communication, values, decision making, religion, politics, science, technology, health, disease, mass media, current events, and cultures and customs of the world.

These are subjects that even the youngest of children can easily think about and relate to in their own lives and experiences, and topics that teachers, even early childhood teachers, can and do easily incorporate into their work. With increased awareness of the importance of these topics to healthy growth and development and of their interconnectedness to sexuality (if only as a foundation for later, more sexuality-specific learning), all early childhood teachers can become effective health and sexuality educators. Indeed, one of the kindergarten teachers in the project became so enamored of the richness of these topics that she eventually chose health and sexuality as the core curriculum for her class for the entire school year—including math!

Once more confident from a philosophical perspective, the teachers were anxious to cut their teeth on actual teaching skills. To identify helpful resources, and to gain experience in answering children's questions about sexuality and reproduction, the group read and formally reviewed more than two dozen books, gathered from school and public libraries, personal collections, and nearby bookstores, that were written for young children about the facts of life. The activity helped the teachers to become increasingly comfortable with the language of sex and reproduction and to generate strategies for dealing with discomfort in the classroom (either their own or the students'). It also facilitated lively discussion about the most appropriate ways to sequence information, particularly about the increasingly sensitive and sophisticated concepts of pregnancy and fetal development, labor and delivery, and intercourse and conception. Perhaps most important, it gave the teachers an important confidence boost. As seasoned teachers and early childhood experts in their own right, they found much to comment on, praise, and criticize in each of the books they reviewed, demonstrating to themselves that this subject of sexuality was not quite so mystifying or difficult after all. Good teaching is good teaching, they realized, and transferable to this topic as well as all others.

Building a Curriculum

Convinced and confident, teachers moved on to the curriculum-building phase of the project. Teachers at each grade selected one or more core health topics that would become the focus of their program for the coming year. They eventually determined, however, that the individual topic or topics chosen were not as important as how well they "fit": Teachers were encouraged to pick topics that would be of special interest to students at their grade level, that could be tied easily to the science concepts and activities also being developed, and that would enable teachers to introduce an aspect of sexuality education in a way that was age appropriate for the students and comfortable for the teacher. One of the kindergarten teachers, for example, selected a study of body parts (including the genitals), discussions of gender and gender roles, and a unit on the five sensory systems as a way of tying the functions of the body to the notion of scientific exploration. Two others decided to focus on nutrition, exercise, and healthy choices with a year-long program in yoga instruction as the centerpiece. They also arranged for a new mother to bring her baby to the class at regular intervals so that the children could observe and chart the baby's development.

It was ultimately the first-grade teachers who were able to develop and carry through the most comprehensive health and sexuality curriculum pieces that came out of the project, probably because they were all in attendance during the summer workshop and were readily able to give one another continuing support.

The Young Child as Scientist

In developing their new science curriculum during the summer project, first-grade teachers made continuous use of the book *The Young Child as Scientist* by Christine Chaille and Lory Britain. These early childhood experts believe that young children act as scientists—by continually asking questions, devising theories, and using observation and experimentation to construct their knowledge about the world. The role of the teacher, then, is to provide an environment in which children will employ these steps spontaneously and to answer children's questions with other questions that will encourage them to further create an answer or theory on their own. In designing the health component of the curriculum, it was therefore important for teachers in the first grade to allow for hands-on experiences and for the encouragement and acceptance of question asking and theory building.

Teachers decided to begin the year with a study of living things, using arthropods as the study's focus. As the children captured insects, spiders, caterpillars, centipedes, and other arthropods, habitats had to be created. Creation of aquaria with crayfish and fiddler crabs brought up important questions. What did these creatures need to sustain life? Did they all need the same things or different things? What was good for them? What was not good for them?

Once habitats were created, long-term captivity provided opportunities for close observation of behavior, changes, bodies, and movement. The creatures' life cycles were scrutinized and discussed, and the subject of mating was opened up. Male and female body parts were discussed openly using correct terminology. When the opportunity arose, mating was observed, eggs were found, and elimination of body wastes was watched. Throughout the study of arthropods the teachers kept track of broader essential understanding about living things, with an eye to future discussions about human bodies, and worked toward that end constantly. In addition, the teachers consciously created an environment in which words with sexual import were used in authentic and natural ways and asking questions of any sort was accepted and encouraged.

Creating a Logical and Comfortable Context for Learning

As a result of the groundwork laid by the first-grade teachers, the actual move to the study of the human body was a gradual and natural one. Comparisons of human and arthropod needs, bodies, and behaviors were already an integral part of the study of living things. To jump-start the topic, one teacher began by asking the students to list any questions they might have about the human body. Many hands went up and she wrote down every question. The children posed many thoughtful and surprisingly sophisticated questions and interests that covered virtually every system of the human body, including the reproductive system, and demonstrated the richness and depth of interest young children have in learning about themselves.

Things We Would Like to Know About the Human Body

1. How do we grow?
2. How does our skin stretch?
3. Why is skin different on different people?
4. How and why does our skin get sweaty?
5. How does our hair grow?
6. How do our eyes see?
7. How do blind people know how to read?
8. How do our eyes blink?
9. How do our eyes move?
10. Why are there nostrils in our nose?
11. How do our ears work?
12. How do we move our mouths?
13. How can we talk?
14. Why are our lips a certain shape?
15. How do we lose our teeth?
16. How do we develop new teeth?
17. What is under our teeth?
18. What are our gums made of?
19. How do we breathe?
20. Why does our stomach go in and out when we breathe?
21. How do we suck in air with our mouth?
22. How does blood get around in our bodies?
23. Why doesn't blood rush to our feet when we sit?
24. How does our heart beat?
25. How does our body work?

26. How are our bones attached?
27. How does our neck move?
28. How does our skeleton move?
29. How can we move?
30. How do we walk?
31. How do our toes wiggle?
32. How can we grasp and hang?
33. Why does our foot have splits where our toes are?
34. Why do we always have to chew our food to get it down and where does it go?
35. Why do we need to pass gas?
36. What happens when we get sick and we can't eat but we can still go on?
37. How does our brain know what to think?
38. How does our brain make us think?
39. What's inside our brain?
40. How does our body control itself?
41. How does the egg inside our mom grow?
42. Why don't children have babies?

The teacher, Mrs. T., was amazed and delighted at the children's level of interest, especially in their questions about origins. She later wrote in her notes: "The question toward the end—'How does the egg inside our mom grow?'—created some conversation between the children. I didn't ask for conversation, as we were asking our questions at the time, but the children immediately began sharing their ideas on this. I can't remember everything they said, but these are some of their theories and the gist of what they had to say: 'The egg that is inside your mom grows just a little, and then, with the food she eats, it grows more and more until finally it bursts and a baby hatches.' And the response: 'No, humans are not hatched. The mom doesn't have that kind of egg in her. We just say she has an egg, but she doesn't really.' And in response again: 'In the egg there is a little baby that grows and grows until it is ready to come out. Then it is born. The mom's stomach gets bigger and bigger.'"

The next day the teacher reread the questions to the children in order. As the questions were read, the children created a learning web titled "The Human Body" to organize the questions, a procedure that created an opportunity for the children to think through the functions of different systems in the body. It was challenging for them to figure out which part of the body related to a particular question, and the task created further discussions, questions, and theories. Sometimes a question was put aside and placed on the web for later study.

An important goal for the first-grade teachers was to give students as many opportunities for hands-on experiences and direct observations as possible. When studying arthropods, for example, there was a constant and ample supply of creatures that provided those opportunities. Finding up-close-and-personal opportunities for the human body study, however, was more challenging. There were charts and posters everywhere in sight in every classroom, some of which depicted clothed children with labels connected by arrows to legs, arms, head, and so on. Some displayed outlines of humans with a focus on a particular system. The first-grade classes also shared "Mr. Bones," a human skeleton the size of an adult, and each classroom contained a variety of bones and skulls. Available to all classes was an apron with Velcro body parts that, when placed on a child, corresponded to the location of her or his own body parts. Each classroom also displayed a rich supply of books on the subject, both fiction and nonfiction.

All of these materials were necessary and effective, but they did not engage the children in a hands-on way. Teachers had to create a variety of interactive experiences that would allow the children opportunities to get closer to the workings of the human body. Periodically, for example, parents were invited to a classroom to share their particular areas of expertise with the students. An orthopedic surgeon spoke to the children about bones, joints, and taking care of your body and showed X rays and samples of the many wonders of medical technology, such as knee replacements. During his presentation he used rubber bands to simulate tendons and put a cast on the unbroken arm of his son while he spoke about how to keep bones healthy and safe. In a different class, a dentist parent brought in a skull and models of the mouth and teeth, and in another, students played "Guess the Animal," using a variety of skulls ranging from a cat to a horse and used the interactive three-dimensional computer program ADAM.

After observing Mr. Bones, one class wanted to create a skeleton their own size. After a long discussion, the class decided they needed a child who would be the model of a first-grade skeleton. They made their decision by lining everyone up in order of size and selecting the child, whose name was Emily, from the middle of the line. Emily's body was then traced onto a large piece of paper, and different groups of children created the parts of an Emily-sized skeleton using papier-mâché in very creative ways— over rolled newspaper for longer bones, over a balloon for the skull, and lightly over carefully cut and shaped poster paper for the sternum, pelvis, and other bones. Little bones of the hands and feet were made with cut-up rolled paper. The children were absolutely thrilled when they saw their skeleton together for the first time. When they held it up to Emily and it was exactly her size, they knew they had done a good job.

The other systems of the body were studied according to the interest of the children in each class. In one group, corn flakes, milk, and bananas were put into a zip-lock plastic bag—the stomach—and the students had a great time squeezing the food together just as the stomach would. One student said, "Gross, it looks like vomit!" The first-grade teachers were amazed at how easily each discussion simply glided along on the interest of the students. The students' observations, such as the one just cited, continuously generated questions, discussions, theories, and new topics for thought. Teachers simply listened to comments and questions, often asking questions in response to questions to encourage independent thinking, and looked for opportunities to take on new aspects of the study and to make connections for the students.

All of these experiences set the stage for a comfortable, active, and engaging discussion of the reproductive system. In Mrs. T.'s classroom, where the children had asked so many wonderful questions about the human body—including "How does the egg inside our mom grow?" and "Why don't children have babies?"—it was fortuitous that the mother of one of the students happened to be pregnant and could visit the class several times throughout the human body study. Since she was also a teacher, she knew that correct use of terms such as *vagina, uterus,* and *sperm,* was the expected norm. The children were very interested in the growing size of her abdomen, and some even took her up on her offer to feel her abdomen and the baby moving inside. She created a time line of her pregnancy from fertilization to birth so the class could follow her progress closely, and they also looked at photos of a growing fetus as the pregnancy progressed.

At the same time, each child was asked to make a time line of his or her own growth and development from birth on. Each one made a small chart, with help from parents, and the time line, complete with photos matching each age, was made into a personal book for each child. In addition, the teacher consolidated all of the time lines to create a birth-to-first-grade time chart of stages and activities of human development. With the help of the chart, and after general discussion of other important stages of growth and maturity, the class was able to answer, in a way that they easily understood, the question why children don't have babies.

Communicating with Parents

As mentioned earlier, the first-grade teachers were deeply concerned about how parents would react to open questions, discussions, and language about the human body, especially about the
reproductive system. After many discussions during the summer,
the teachers decided that they should treat this subject in exactly
the same manner as every other curricular topic. Parents would be
informed at a back-to-school night that the science curriculum
would include a study of the human body, that the body parts
would be called by their real names, and that questions and discussions would be carried out in an age-appropriate, sensitive, and
honest way—as all subjects are treated throughout the school.

Across all grade levels in this elementary school, teachers create
an informative and continuous line of communication by writing
letters to their classroom parents each week. It was through these
letters that parents were kept informed about the progress of the
science study, the projects, and previous and upcoming discussions.
Excerpts from these letters from one first-grade teacher provide a
window into the life of the classroom and a model of ongoing
school-family partnerships:

November 1. In the next weeks I plan to move into conversations about how we are like arthropods. After all, we are
living animals, too. This will take us into growth, development and human needs. The subjects of different body systems and functions, such as skeletal, reproductive, and
digestive, may come up, and questions asked by the children
will be discussed openly and frankly, using correct names of
body parts and functions.

January 31. The children have finished their body part
aprons. They are very nice and will come home next week.

Please use them to assess your child's knowledge of the
digestive system and the organs that are on the apron.
I wish you had been in the room while they were cutting
out the parts and gluing them on the aprons. Here are samples of what I heard: "I lost my kidneys!" "*I'm* cutting out
my intestines." "Has anybody seen my liver?" I kept wishing
I had a tape recorder. . . .

The children are very interested in the progress of our
pregnant mother. Because Mrs. Phelps stops by often, the
children have been observing her blossoming abdomen and
have had opportunities to ask her questions. Next week
we'll look at pictures of a growing fetus and talk about the
body parts involved in this system. There have been several
times during our study of the human body when the subject
of how the body changes as it matures has come up. Ages
ago a student asked the question, "Why can't young animals
have babies?" Her question will be answered next week.

February 7. In Science we have had interesting discussions
about the life of a person before he or she is born, or what
kinds of changes occur from conception to birth. The group
had to work to create a list of what happens from the time
human life is just a "speck" until a baby is born.

Of course, we have our time line from birth to the present of a first grader to show development. In our discussions we did talk about the fact that the body changes as
one gets older and some of these changes allow a male and
a female to create a baby. (There's the answer to Jennie's
great question of why a young animal cannot make a baby.)

We talked about the fact that it takes an egg from the
female and a sperm from the male to make a new life, but
not one child asked how these get together. I wonder when
and if that question will be asked? I'll let you know.

February 21. I have pretty much wound up the science study of the human body. Yesterday and today we talked about how all systems work together in the body and why it is important to keep all those working parts healthy. Each child created a list of things we can do to keep our bodies healthy and another list things that are not healthy for our bodies. Between them, the children listed everything from eating properly to exercise to keeping themselves safe and more. They included alcohol, smoking, drugs, and too much coffee on their list of things that are not healthy.

Your children's interest in the human body is at a high level. Throughout the study I have answered their questions honestly and have used proper names for body parts, something I hope you are doing as well. Letting the children know you are open to hearing questions about the body by answering honestly creates a healthy environment for further questions as these come to your child's mind. I have a good book that you might find helpful about answering your child's questions about sex. Let me know if you would like to read it.

Clearly, these letters were not only informative but helped to include and educate the parents as well. Although the February 7th letter mentions the fact that the question "How do the sperm and the egg get together" had not yet been asked, it did eventually come up in two of the four first-grade classrooms. After several weeks of study and work on the human body, while the teacher in one room was reading aloud one day, a child's hand went up, interrupting with some urgency. "There's something I don't understand," asked the child. "How do the sperm from the father get into the mother and to her egg?" In another classroom, a child asked the question in a slightly different way: "I understand the sperm and egg have to meet. How does that happen?" The teacher, who had previously skipped over that part of the story because no child had yet asked that question and she wanted it to come first from the children, asked if anyone else had wondered about it. When other children indicated their interest, she turned back to the page she had skipped and read relevant parts to the children: ". . . the man's penis gets hard so that he can put it into the woman's vagina, then sperm comes out of his penis and goes through the vagina and into an egg."

The other teacher also asked if anyone else had wondered about that question and if anyone would like to answer it for the class. A girl raised her hand and explained, "The man puts his penis into the woman. The sperm leaves the penis and finds the egg." Both teachers asked if there were any more questions, and when there were none, went on reading. In both classes there was a bit of giggling and an occasional "yuck." Each teacher explained that this was an adult activity, that children did not engage in this behavior, because they were not physically ready to, and that when they became older they would probably become more interested. This comment seemed to settle down those children who had felt uncomfortable.

In each case, the teacher called the parents of the child who had asked the question to prepare them in case the subject came up again at home. The teacher explained what the child had asked, the context in which the topic was being studied, and how the question had been answered. Parents seemed most interested in hearing how the answer had been presented. No other parents called the teachers.

In the other two classrooms the children did not ask "the question" but seemed satisfied with the statement that the sperm and egg meet to create a baby. Although there were discussions during the arthropod study about exactly how the process occurs, the children did not ask about it during the human body study. It's also interesting to note that Mrs. T., the teacher whose letters are quoted above, did not, in the end, feel it necessary to tell the parents that the question had been asked, because, when it finally was asked and answered, the process felt so normal and usual that there seemed no need to single it out.

The teachers realized that the key to their success with the parents was keeping them well informed before and during the entire human body study. Communicating with parents in a matter-of-fact manner gave them opportunities to deal with the subject at home in the same honest and open way that they knew it would be dealt with at school. None of the first-grade teachers was challenged or questioned in any negative way about their units in the classroom. In fact, parents seemed very comfortable with its being part of the first-grade curriculum and with the fact that it was being treated in an open and honest way. The study of the human body became as much a team effort between parents and teachers as it is with all other subjects.

Ingredients for Success

There are many "active ingredients" that enabled this wonderful program to evolve and thrive. Foremost was the uncompromising dedication of the teachers involved to meeting the real developmental needs and interests of children—even when these initially seemed at odds with the needs of adults. Second was certainly the inherent strengths of this particular school as an educational institution, including its superb teaching staff, an informed and engaged parent body, and an administration and board of trustees willing to trust and stand behind their faculty, their commitment to children, and their own carefully framed philosophy. Crucial as well was the opportunity for adequate training and preparation for all personnel involved.

The many positive outcomes of the program were evidence of its success: a creative, effective, and integrated curriculum; an enthusiastic, gratified, and increasingly confident faculty; receptive and appreciative parents; and most important, comfortable and competent young children who have been given a solid, healthy foundation in the basics of sexual literacy. It is truly remarkable that these same curricular pieces, put in place here for students at the early childhood level, are rarely in existence even at the upper elementary levels in most schools throughout the country. In fact, one of the ongoing effects of the program—and the "can do" attitude embraced by its early childhood staff—has been an ever increasing interest in health and sexuality education at the school among its own upper-elementary teachers.

Public Schools Can Be Responsive and Responsible

Most certainly, the fact that the setting for this program was a small, relatively homogeneous private school rather than a large public institution or school district was also part of this picture. Independent school educators typically face fewer layers of bureaucracy and accountability—and tend to enjoy greater freedom and flexibility—than their public school counterparts. However, please don't mistake this for a fundamentally public-private issue: Parents need to know that *any* school community with a steadfast commitment to understanding and meeting real developmental needs, public or private, can be successful.

The state of New Jersey is one clear case in point where in the mid-1990s a unique demonstration program took place in elementary schools in fourteen school districts throughout the state. Under the guidance of the acclaimed New Jersey Network for Family Life Education, specially trained teachers implemented portions of a family life curriculum specifically designed for kindergarten through third-grade classrooms. In nearly all cases, parents were supportive, teachers gained important expertise and confidence, and children demonstrated clear, steady growth in knowledge and comfort that greatly facilitated their learning of increasingly sophisticated topics presented in the later grades. In addition, sexual misbehavior—such as name-calling, rumors, intimidation, and inappropriate touching—diminished.

Parents should not have to be the lone voice in their children's lives delivering sage, healthy, and ongoing sexual guidance. Schools need to hear routinely from parents who understand, support, and expect truly age-appropriate and comprehensive sexuality education, not just from those who are opposed. Children of all ages need and deserve for all of us—schools and families—to embrace these challenges and to forge successful partnerships with one another.

8

Resources for Parents, Caretakers, and Teachers

For further reading and exploration of the topic of childhood sexuality education, you'll find these resources interesting and enlightening.

For the Family Bookshelf

Judy Cyprian, *Teaching Human Sexuality: A Guide for Parents and Other Caretakers* (Annapolis Junction, MD: Child Welfare League of America, 1998); for foster parents especially.

Ronald Moglia and Jon Knowles, eds., *All About Sex: A Family Resource on Sex and Sexuality* (New York: Planned Parenthood Federation of America, 1997).

Marcia Quackenbush and Sylvia Villarreal, *Educating Young Children about AIDS* (Santa Cruz, CA: ETR Associates, 1992).

Karin Schwier and Dave Hingsburger, *Sexuality: Your Sons and Daughters with Intellectual Disabilities* (Baltimore, MD: Brookes Publishing, 2000).

On Parenting

Anne Bernstein, *Flight of the Stork: What Children Think (and When) about Sex and Family Building* (Indianapolis, IN: Perspectives Press, 1994.

Toni Cavanagh Johnson, *Understanding Your Child's Sexual Behavior: What's Natural and Healthy* (Oakland, CA: New Harbinger Publications, 1999).

Deborah M. Roffman, *Sex and Sensibility: The Thinking Parent's Guide to Talking Sense About Sex* (Cambridge, MA: Perseus Publishing, 2001).

Pamela Wilson, *When Sex Is the Subject: Attitudes and Answers for Young Children* (Santa Cruz, CA: ETR Associates, 1991).

For Young Children

You'll want to read these yourself before deciding to share them with your children.

Lois Abramchik, *Is Your Family like Mine?* (New York: Open Heart, Open Mind Publishing, 1993).

Laurie Krasny Brown and Marc Brown, *What's the Big Secret? Talking About Sex with Girls and Boys* (New York: Little, Brown, 1997).

Joanna Cole, *How You Were Born* (New York: Morrow Junior Books, 1993).

Debra Frasier, *On the Day You Were Born.* (New York: Harcourt Brace, 1997).

Lory Freeman, *It's My Body: A Book to Teach Young Children How to Resist Uncomfortable Touch* (Seattle, WA: Parenting Press, 1982).

Linda Girard, *You Were Born on Your Very First Birthday* (Niles, IL: Albert Whitman, 1992).

Sol Gordon and Judith Gordon, *Did the Sun Shine Before You Were Born?* (Amherst, NY: Prometheus Books, 1990).

Robie Harris, *Happy Birth Day!* (Cambridge, MA: Candlewick Press, 1996).

Robie Harris, *It's So Amazing: A Book About Eggs, Sperm, Birth, Babies, and Families* (New York: Penguin Putnam, 1999).

Gina Inoglia, *Look Inside Your Body* (New York: Putnam, 1989).

Mary Knight, *Welcoming Babies* (Gardiner, ME: Tilbury House Publications, 1998).

Phoebe Koehler, *The Day We Met You* (New York: Simon and Schuster, 1990).

Susan Meredith, *Where Do Babies Come From?* (Tulsa, OK: EDC Publishing, 1991).

Leslea Newman, *Heather Has Two Mommies* (Los Angeles, CA: Alyson Publications, 1989).

Lennart Nilson and Katarina Swanberg, *How Was I Born?* (New York: Bantam, 1996).

Patricia Pearse and Edwina Riddel, *See How You Grow: A Lift the Flap Body Book* (New York: Barron's Educational Series, 1988).

Mark Shoen, *Belly Buttons Are Navels* (New York: Prometheus Books, 1990).

Kathy Stinson, *Bare Naked Book* (Buffalo, NY: Firefly Books, 1988).

Michael Willhoite, *Daddy's Roommate* (Los Angeles, CA: Alyson Publications, 1991).

Videos

Raising Healthy Kids: Families Talk About Sexual Health. Family Health Productions, P.O. Box 1799, Gloucester, MA 01931-1799; (978) 282–9970; www.abouthealth.com.

Talking About Sex: A Guide For Families: Planned Parenthood Federation of America (see listing below).

Organizations

Parents, Families, and Friends of Lesbians and Gays (PFLAG), 1726 M Street, NW, Suite 400, Washington, DC 20036; (202) 467-8180; www.pflag.org.

Planned Parenthood Federation of America, 810 Seventh Avenue, New York, NY 10019; (212) 541-7800; www.plannedparenthood.org.

The Sexuality Information and Education Council of the United States (SIECUS), 130 West 42nd Street, Suite 350, New York, NY 10036-7802; (212) 819-9770; www.siecus.org.

Basic Facts All Adults Should Know

Organs, Systems, and Openings

In my teaching I'm constantly amazed at how little children and adolescents know about the bodies they inhabit. As soon as children learn to talk, it's important for us to begin teaching them about their bodies and how they work, and we should take care to label sexual body parts, just as all others, with correct, matter-of-fact terminology. As children approach three or four, we can also begin to educate them about the fact that bodies have an *inside* and an *outside* and that many of our parts—or *organs*—are located where we can't see them. An easy way to teach this concept is to help them understand what happens to their food after they swallow it and can't see it anymore. (There are many clever and engaging big-picture books available in stores and public libraries that show and educate about the internal parts of the body).

Gradually, we'll also be able to explain that each organ inside our body is connected to other organs and that, together, certain groups of organs make up each of our various *body systems*. We have many different body systems, and in each one a group of different organs works together to do a particular job that helps keep our body alive and healthy. Once children have grasped this concept, we'll be in a good position eventually to fit the reproductive system right into the body along with all the others—making it ever so much easier to talk and learn about. The conversation won't be about SEX! but simply a continuation of many earlier low-key and matter-of-fact discussions about how our bodies work.

Another really helpful concept to teach young children concerns their *body openings:* We have several places on the outside of our body that lead to certain organs on the inside, and it is through these openings (please don't say *holes!*) that things from the outside go in and other important things from the inside go out. With very little effort, adults can use many different everyday experiences to reinforce this idea. These basic anatomical concepts will also make it much easier for us to explain the mechanics of intercourse and birth later on.

Be sure to explain as well that girls and women have *three* of these opening in the area between their legs—the *urinary, vaginal,* and *anal* openings—and that these openings are connected to tubes, organs, and systems (the *urinary, digestive,* and *reproductive*) that are *not connected either structurally or functionally.*

Stomachs, Abdomens, and Uteruses

Food and stomachs are very real to children and easy for them to understand. Unless we are very careful in how we speak to them when they are young, they will grow up thinking that their stomach, their belly or abdomen (which is nothing but a space or cavity), and their abdominal wall (the wall of muscle, fat, and skin in front of the abdomen) are one and the same. This sloppy terminology—*especially if we also tell children at some point that babies grow in stomachs or bellies*—sets them up for untold confusion later on.

By late elementary school, most of the students I teach have no conception of their abdomen as a space in which many organs and parts of different body systems are located. As a result, they picture the various parts of the reproductive, urinary, and digestive systems hopelessly intertwined. Since what they learn the earliest is often what they remember the longest, what I try to reteach them may or may not stick. Not surprisingly, when I see them in the classroom again two or three years later, often their understanding has reverted to their earlier learning. When it comes time to discuss fetal development, it becomes clear that many even think the umbilical cord is connected directly form baby's stomach to mother's!

Vaginas and Vulvas

An even more fundamental confusion exists in the minds of most girls and boys and probably many adult men and women: The vagina, contrary to popular opinion, is *not* located on the *outside* of the female anatomy. The vagina is an *internal* pouch—really just a "potential" space located just inside the vaginal opening—whereas the *vulva* is the collective name for all of the *external* female genitalia, which include the inner and outer labia (or vaginal "lips"), the clitoris, and the mons (the mound of skin on top of the pubic bone where pubic hair eventually grows). Thinking that the vagina is located somewhere on the outside or that it is both inside *and* outside, as many people do, is tantamount to not knowing the difference between your face and your throat!

Many girls and women, in fact, have never even heard the word *vulva* and can barely name any of the organs that compose it. This ignorance of girls' and women's bodies and of the names that describe them harkens to the days when women's organs were considered "dirty" and shameful. And, since the function of these organs is primarily sexual and not reproductive, it also reflects a time in our history when "good" and "normal" girls and women were considered incapable of sexual feelings—*ever*. Is it a sad fact that many young girls and teenagers even today feel and act as if these parts of their bodies are like foreign objects about which they often feel uncomfortable and even ashamed.

Males Have Reproductive Parts, Too

For the thirty years that I've been teaching, it's been clear that neither males nor females know much at all about the internal male parts. I think this lack of information derives from a time when most "sex education" was really "period education"; as a result, many adults have never really been required to formally learn about the male reproductive system. Even today, the children and adolescents that I teach—both girls and boys—are often incredibly confused about such basic concepts as the difference between sperm and semen, or erections and ejaculations. And terms such as *vas deferens, seminal vesicle,* and *prostate gland* (an organ which is mentioned frequently in the news today) are not even in their memory banks. It's interesting and, I think, quite revealing that many of us seem to know *the most* about internal female organs (which are about reproduction) and external male organs (which are about sexual pleasure) and *the least* about female external organs (which are about pleasure) and male internal organs (which are about reproduction). Clearly, we need to be doing a better job of educating *everybody* about *everything.*

The Reproduction and Sexual Response Systems

The reproductive system is unique among all other body systems: (1) As individuals, each of us only has *half* of a system; (2) the half system we do have is totally nonfunctional for the first several years of our lives, as well as the last years (at least for women); (3) even during the years in which the system is working, we can survive quite well (as individuals) if we don't ever use it! These three features are a great opening for discussing myriad sexual and reproductive facts—intercourse, conception, puberty, menopause, and sexual and reproductive decision making to name a few.

A related system—the sexual response system—is much more straightforward though even less well understood. Although, like the reproductive system, the sexual response system is not necessary for individual survival, unlike the reproductive system, it is fully present and functional at birth. It greatly surprises most adults, and young people, too, to learn this basic biological fact. Perhaps it would help us better integrate and talk about the sexual parts of our lives if we came to accept our sexual system as simply another of our body's basic functions. In truth, babies' bodies are quite capable of sexual feelings, even to the point of orgasm. Baby boys experience frequent erections, and in baby girls, sexual lubrication regularly passes through the walls of the vagina. Indeed, both of these reactions occur involuntarily during sleep throughout our entire lives. And though only males ejaculate, both male and female bodies, when sexually aroused, experience roughly the same sequence of physiological events and body sensations (referred to in the sexology literature as *excitement, plateau, orgasm,* and *resolution*) known as the "sexual response cycle."

Acknowledgments

There are many people whose input and support have been crucial to the publication of this book.

I am indebted most especially to the superb educators with whom I was privileged to work in the 1996 Faculty and Curricular Advancement (FACA) project on early childhood science education at The Park School of Baltimore: Peter Babcox, Hillary Barry, Susan Benedict, Megan Ford, Carol Kinne, Susan Koh, Rob Piper, Noreen Potempa, Karleen Tyksinski, and Melpa Warres. Special thanks to Megan for helping me to sharpen my thinking about young learners, and to Karleen for her enthusiasm and creativity and for recording and sharing so generously the progress in her classroom, thereby providing a unique, invaluable opportunity to witness and understand the sexual learning/teaching process.

Much credit and gratitude go as well to Louise Mehta, associate head of The Park School and director of the FACA program; David Jackson, head of The Park School; Betsy Leighton, principal of the Lower School; and Hillary Jacobs, director of advancement; for their unfailing encouragement and support.

To the staffs of The Center for Family Life Education in Hackensack, New Jersey, and of The New Jersey Network for Family Life Education, I wish to offer my gratitude and praise for your pioneering work in the field of early childhood sexuality education, with special thanks to Peggy Brick, Susan Wilson, and Bill Taverner. I think I speak for all of us in acknowledging, as well, the special contributions of our mutual and longtime colleague Pamela

Wilson, also a dedicated and talented pioneer in the field of sexuality education for young children. Kudos also for the library staff at the Sexuality Information and Education Council of the United States (SIECUS) and the Planned Parenthood Federation of America, for maintaining such marvelous collections and for their very able research assistance.

To Kathy Levin Shapiro, Josh Roffman, Joanne Mason, Linda Butler, Bonnie Bain, and Melpa Warres, who read all or parts of the manuscript, please know how very much your comments and suggestions helped to improve and enhance this work.

As always, my heartfelt thanks and abiding respect go to my literary agent, Gail Ross, and to my editor, Marnie Cochran, and publicist, Lissa Warren, both at Perseus Publishing. They continue to make all things possible.

References

Anne Bernstein, *Flight of the Stork: What Children Think (and When) About Sex and Family Building* (Indianapolis: Perspective Press, 1994).

Ernest Borneman, *Childhood Phases of Maturity* (Amherst, NY: Prometheus Books, 1994).

T. Berry Brazelton, *Toddlers and Parents: A Declaration of Independence* (New York: Dell Publishing, 1989).

T. Berry Brazelton and Joshua D. Sparrow, *Touchpoints Three to Six: Your Child's Emotional and Behavioral Development* (Cambridge, MA: Perseus Publishing, 2001).

Sue Bredekamp and Teresa Rosegant, eds., *Reaching Potentials: Transforming Early Childhood Curriculum and Assessment* (Washington, DC: National Association for the Education of Young Children, 1995).

Peggy Brick, Nan Davis, Maxine Fischel, Trudie Lupo, Ann MacVicar, and Jean Marshall, *Bodies, Birth, and Babies: Sexuality Education in Early Childhood Programs* (Hackensack, NJ: The Center for Family Life Education, Planned Parenthood of Bergen County, 1989).

Peggy Brick, Sue Montfort, and Nancy Blume, *Healthy Foundations: The Teacher's Book—Responding to Young Children's Questions and Behaviors Regarding Sexuality* (Hackensack, NJ: The Center for Family Life Education, Planned Parenthood of Greater Northern New Jersey, 1993).

Christine Chaille and Lory Britain, *The Young Child as Scientist* (New York: Harper Collins, 1994.)

Early Childhood Sexuality Education Task Force, *Right from the Start* (New York: Sexuality Information and Education Council of the United States, 1995).

David Finkelhor, "The Prevention of Child Sexual Abuse: An Overview of Needs and Problems," *SIECUS Report* 8, no. 1 (September 1984): 1–5.

William N. Friedrich, Jennifer Fisher, Daniel Broughton, Margaret Houston, and Constance R. Shafran, "Normative Sexual Behavior in Children: A Contemporary Sample," *Pediatrics* 101, no. 4 (April 1989): 1–8.

Margie J. Geasler, Linda L. Dannison, and Connie J. Edlund, "Sexuality Education of Young Children: Parental Concerns," *Family Relations* 44 (April 1995): 184–188.

Jean Gochros, *What to Say After You Clear Your Throat* (Kailua, HI: Press Pacifica, 1980.

Susan Golombok, *Gender Development* (New York: Cambridge University Press, 1994).

Patricia Hoertdoerfer, *The Parent Guide to Our Whole Lives: Grades K–1 and 4–6* (Boston: Unitarian Universalist Association, 2000).

Toni Cavanaugh Johnson, *Understanding Your Child's Sexual Behavior: What's Natural and Healthy* (Oakland, CA: New Harbinger Publications, 1999).

Frederick Kaeser, Claudia Di Salvo, and Ron Moglia, "Sexual Behaviors of Young Children That Occur in Schools," *Journal of Sex Education and Therapy* 25, no. 4 (2000): 277–285.

Joanne B. Koch and Linda N. Freeman, *Good Parents for Hard Times: Raising Responsible Kids in the Age of Drug Use and Early Sexual Activity* (New York: Fireside, 1992).

Penelope Leach, *Babyhood* (New York: Alfred A. Knopf, 2000).

Alicia F. Lieberman, *The Emotional Life of the Toddler* (New York: Free Press, 1993).

Sue Montfort, Peggy Brick, and Nancy Blume, *Healthy Foundations: Developing Positive Policies and Programs Regarding Young Children's Learning about Sexuality* (Hackensack, NJ: The Center for Family Life Education, Planned Parenthood of Greater Northern New Jersey, 1993).

Wardell B. Pomeroy, *Your Child and Sex* (New York: Delacorte Press, 1974).

Elizabeth J. Roberts, ed., *Childhood Sexual Learning: The Unwritten Curriculum* (Cambridge, MA: Ballinger Publishing, 1980).

F. J. Rutherford, *Benchmarks for Science Literacy* (New York: Oxford University Press, 1993).

Seattle-King County Department of Public Health, *All About Life: K–4 Sexuality Curriculum* (Seattle, WA: Seattle-King County Department of Public Health, 1995).

Ann Schurrman, *Baby Steps: Implementing Family Life Education Programs in the Early Grades* (New Brunswick, NJ: Network for Family Life Education, Rutgers the State University of New Jersey, 1997).

Marilyn Segal, *Your Child at Play: Three to Five Years* (New York: New Market Press, 1998).

Study Group of New York, *Children and Sex: The Parents Speak* (New York: Facts on File, 1983).

Wisconsin Department of Public Instruction, *A Guide to Curriculum Planning in Health Education* (Milwaukee, WI: Wisconsin Department of Public Instruction, 1994).

Chip Wood, *Yardsticks: Children in the Classroom, Ages 4–14: A Resource for Parents and Teachers* (Greenfield, MA: Northeast Foundation for Children, 1997).